NORMANDY

FIONA DUNCAN & LEONIE GLASS

DK

EYEWITNESS TRAVEL

Left **Caudebec-en-Caux** Right **Canoeing on the Risle**

LONDON, NEW YORK,
MELBOURNE, MUNICH AND DELHI
www.dk.com

Produced by DP Services,
31 Ceylon Road, London W14 0PY

Reproduced by Colourscan, Singapore
Printed and bound in China by Leo Paper Products
Ltd

First published in Great Britain in 2004 by
Dorling Kindersley Limited
80 Strand, London WC2R 0RL

12 13 14 15 10 9 8 7 6 5 4 3 2 1

Reprinted with revisions 2006, 2008, 2010, 2012

Copyright 2004, 2012 ©
Dorling Kindersley Limited, London
A Penguin Company

A CIP catalogue record is available from
the British Library.

ISBN: 978-1-40537-040-0

Within each Top 10 list in this book, no hierarchy of
quality or popularity is implied. All 10 are, in the
editor's opinion, of roughly equal merit.

MIX
Paper from
responsible sources
FSC™ C018179
www.fsc.org

Contents

Normandy's Top 10

The information in this DK Eyewitness Top 10 Travel Guide is checked regularly.
Every effort has been made to ensure that this book is as up-to-date as possible at the time of
going to press. Some details, however, such as telephone numbers, opening hours, prices,
gallery hanging arrangements and travel information are liable to change. The publishers
cannot accept responsibility for any consequences arising from the use of this book, nor for
any material on third party websites, and cannot guarantee that any website address in this
book will be a suitable source of travel information. We value the views and suggestions of
our readers very highly. Please write to: Publisher, DK Eyewitness Travel Guides,
Dorling Kindersley, 80 Strand, London WC2R 0RL, Great Britain, or email: travelguides@dk.com.

Cover: Front - **AWL Images**: Doug Pearson main; **Dorling Kindersley**: Mike Dunning bl. Spine - **Dorling
Kindersley**: Max Alexander b. Back - **Dorling Kindersley**: Max Alexander ca; Tony Souter cra; **Photoshot/
World Pictures**: Nicholas Holt ca.

Left **Pays de Caux** Right **Honfleur**

Around Normandy

Streetsmart

Contents

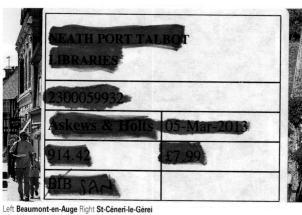

Left **Beaumont-en-Auge** Right **St-Céneri-le-Gérei**

 Following pages **Le Vieux Bassin, Honfleur harbour**

NORMANDY'S
TOP 10

NORMANDY'S TOP 10

﹖10 Normandy Highlights

Normandy brings a dozen different images to mind: William the Conqueror, the D-Day landings, Mont-St-Michel; the bleak landscape of the Cotentin coast, the sparkling summertime playground of the Côte Fleurie; sumptuous châteaux, historic abbeys, famous gardens; the orchards of the Auge, the picture-postcard scenery of the Suisse Normande; Monet's home at Giverny, the Cabourg immortalized by Proust – or perhaps it's cider, calvados and camembert. Whatever your list, it will barely scratch the surface of this rich and rewarding region.

Mont-St-Michel
Now iconic in its fame, this solitary rock dominated by its monumental abbey became a place of pilgrimage when St Aubert built an oratory here over 1,000 years ago *(see pp8–11)*.

Bayeux Tapestry

Unique historical document; astonishing work of art. The Tapestry tells the story of the Norman Conquest of England in 1066 *(see pp12–15)*.

Honfleur
A magnet for artists today as it has been since the 19th century, this picturesque maritime town was also an important centre of trade *(see pp16–17)*.

Abbaye de Jumièges
These magnificent, eerie ruins – a subtle blend of Romanesque and Gothic architecture – are the remains of the Benedictine abbey founded by St Philibert in the 7th century *(see pp18–19)*.

Rouen Cathedral

It took nearly 400 years to build this splendid monument to the Gothic style, from the beautifully harmonious nave to the ornately carved west front *(see pp20–23)*.

Caen

Old and new happily cohabit in this lively, cultured regional capital, still dominated by William the Conqueror's Château Ducal and his two great abbeys *(see pp24–5)*.

Deauville and La Côte Fleurie

The string of resorts on this lovely stretch of Normandy's coastline creates a summer paradise. Racy and romantic, Deauville is a magnet for glamorous visitors *(see pp26–7)*.

D-Day Beaches

The Allied landings of June 1944 and the Battle of Normandy that followed are movingly commemorated in museums, memorials and cemeteries throughout the area *(see pp28–31)*.

Pays d'Auge

Quintessential Normandy, famous for its cider, its cheese, its gently rolling landscape, its orchards, and its half-timbered manor houses *(see pp32–3)*.

Giverny

The house where Monet lived and worked for more than 40 years, and the stunning garden he created using flowers as his palette are a tribute to the great painter *(see pp34–7)*.

TOP10 Mont-St-Michel

One of the most spectacular sights in Normandy, this craggy rock crowned by a magnificent abbey appears to erupt from the surrounding landscape – a broad expanse of sand or sea, depending on the dramatic tides. The region's star attraction since pilgrims first flocked here 1,000 years ago, it now draws some three million visitors each year – and has perhaps 50 true inhabitants.

View of Mont-St-Michel

🍽 **Cafés and restaurants line the Grande Rue.**

🚶 **Contact Chemins de la Baie (02 33 89 80 88) for a guided bay walk from Genêts to Mont-St-Michel.**

- Map B5
- Office du Tourisme: blvd de l'Avancée. 02 33 60 14 30
- Abbey: 02 33 89 80 00. Open May–Aug: 9am–7pm; Sep–Apr: 9:30am–5pm. Adm charge
- Musée Historique: 02 33 60 07 01. Open 9am–6pm daily. Adm charge
- Logis Tiphaine. 02 33 60 23 34. Open 9am–6pm daily. Adm charge
- Archéoscope: 02 33 89 01 85. Open mid-Feb–mid-Sep: 9:30am–5pm. Adm charge
- Scriptorial d'Avranches: pl d'Estouteville, 50300 Avranches. 02 33 79 57 00. Open Jul–Aug: 10am–7pm; Feb–Dec: varies. Adm charge
- Ecomusée de la Baie du Mont Saint-Michel: rte de Grouin du Sud, 50300 Vains. 02 33 89 06 06. Open Apr–Jun: 2–6pm; Jul–Aug: 10am–7pm. Adm charge

Top 10 Features

1. Abbey
2. Ramparts
3. Grande Rue
4. Musée Historique
5. Logis Tiphaine
6. Archéoscope
7. Église St-Pierre
8. Chapelle St-Aubert
9. Scriptorial d'Avranches
10. Ecomusée de la Baie du Mont Saint-Michel

1 Abbey

This splendid building *(above right)* is a pleasing jumble of architectural styles. Its jewel is the Merveille, built during the abbey's heyday and incorporating cloisters, knights' hall, refectory and guests' room.

2 Ramparts

Punctuated by imposing towers, the longest section was built to repel the English during the Hundred Years' War. The abbot's soldiers lodged in the Tour de l'Arcade *(above)*.

3 Grande Rue

Through the fortified Porte du Roy, its portcullis still visible, the Grande Rue *(below)* winds steeply uphill. Pretty and cobbled, it was the 12th-century pilgrim's way, and remains a route to the top – though now you have to run a gauntlet of souvenir shops and over-priced restaurants.

➔ *A project is under way to replace the causeway to the island with a dam that allows the river and tides to scour away accumulated silt.*

Musée Historique

Highlights are the garden periscope, 14th-century monks' bath *(above)*, 17th-century riding boots, and recreation of the prisons.

Logis Tiphaine

Chief of the king's armies Bertrand du Guesclin built this house in 1365 for his wife, Tiphaine – a safe haven while he was away at war.

Entrance

Archéoscope

A large model of the Mont rises from a huge tank of water in a spectacle of sound and light, with a historical commentary in English.

Église St-Pierre

The most interesting feature of the parish church, begun in the 11th century but not completed until the 17th, is the apse that straddles a narrow street. Its treasures include a silver statue of St Michael.

Chapelle St-Aubert

Legend tells of a huge rock blocking the entrance to a cave where the abbey now stands. Nobody could move it until a small boy miraculously pushed it into the sea with his foot. This tiny 15th-century chapel *(right)* was built on the site where the rock was supposed to have landed.

Scriptorial d'Avranches

Films and games lead visitors through a celebration of the written word, from beautifully illuminated medieval manuscripts to modern e-books. ❧ *Map B5*

Ecomusée de la Baie du Mont Saint-Michel

This child-friendly exploration centre, set in a farm complex on the coast, has models and interactive displays showcasing the environment and wildlife of the bay, along with its history of fishing and salt production. ❧ *Map B5*

Tides

Mont-St-Michel has the highest tides in continental Europe, with a difference of up to 15 m (49 ft) between low and high water in March and September, when the spring tides occur. When the tide is out, it exposes around 250 sq km (97 sq miles) of sand. The tide is also unusually strong, running across the flat expanse of sand at a speed of some 10 kph (6 mph). The strongest tides occur two days after a full or new moon, when the sea reaches its highest level at 8 or 9 am and pm.

For more on St Michael **See page 11**

Left **Cloisters** Centre **Abbey Church** Right **Refectory**

🔟 Mont-St-Michel: Abbey Features

Key

▓	Church Level
▓	Middle Level

1 West Terrace
From this terrace, there are breathtaking views over the bay. On a clear day, you can see as far as the Channel Islands – the source of the granite used to build the abbey.

2 Abbey Church
Despite its fine roof, the austere Romanesque nave – the oldest part of the church – is eclipsed by the glorious Flamboyant Gothic chancel. The walls inside the west front are still scorched from a 19th-century prison fire.

3 Cloisters
A garden enclosed by a double row of delicate pink granite columns, the cloisters gave the monks a place to meditate, converse and exercise.

4 Refectory
Apart for one who would read aloud from the Scriptures, the monks ate their meals in silence in this unusual room, which has rows of narrow side windows invisible from the entrance.

5 Guests' Room
Light floods through large windows into this elegant rib-vaulted room used to receive important guests. Food was cooked in the two huge fireplaces.

6 Crypt of the Mighty Pillars
To support the new chancel, 10 massive pillars were built in this 15th-century crypt, a waiting room for those anticipating the judgement of the abbot, who presided over the Belle-Chaise courtroom next door.

7 St Martin's Crypt
Decorated with frescoes, this crypt, which provided the foundation for the south transept, was the funeral chapel for lay people.

8 Prison
During the Revolution, the abbey was used as a prison. The iron cage used to confine dangerous prisoners is long gone, but the vast wheel for hoisting up provisions is still in place.

9 Knights' Hall
This vast, imposing hall was the monks' *scriptorium*, where they studied and copied manuscripts. A wooden trap door led to the food store.

10 St Etienne's Chapel
The monks' funeral chapel was well placed between the infirmary and the ossuary, where the bones of the dead were preserved. Monks kept vigil over the dead for three days and nights.

Top 10 Events in the History of Mont-St-Michel

St Michael and St Aubert

According to legend, St Michael, the archangel, appeared three times in a dream to Aubert, Bishop of Avranches, commanding him to build an oratory on Mont Tombe (tomb on the hill). When Aubert delayed, the impatient archangel prodded a finger into Aubert's forehead, leaving a dent. Aubert's church rapidly became a centre of pilgrimage for the miquelots, followers of the cult of St Michael, which had taken root in the West in the 5th century. The brightly gilded statue on top of the abbey spire, sculpted in 1897 by Emmanuel Frémiet, portrays the archangel in traditional fashion (below). Armour-clad, he is slaying a dragon (symbol of the devil) with his sword. In his other hand he carries a set of scales – a reference to the medieval belief that it was his role to weigh the souls on Judgment Day.

Saint Michael
The Archangel Michael is the warlike angel of the Apocalypse, who slays the devil – in the form of a dragon – in the great conflict at the end of time. In Normandy, he is the patron saint of mariners.

St Michael defeating the dragon above Mont-St-Michel

For more on Norman abbeys See pp46–7

11

🔟 Bayeux Tapestry

Both a unique historical document and an astonishing work of art, the Bayeux Tapestry tells the story of the Norman Conquest of England in 1066 – and it tells it with thrilling narrative drive. Stitched in eight brilliant shades of red, yellow and blue wool, the 58 strip-cartoon-style scenes were embroidered just 11 years after the Conquest onto a single 230 ft (70 m) linen cloth – at the behest, it is thought, of William the Conquerer's half-brother Odo, Bishop of Bayeux. It is displayed in a renovated seminary, along with helpful explanatory exhibitions.

Museum façade

🍽 For an excellent lunch, try Le Pommier, rue des Cuisiniers, or Le P'tit Resto, 2 rue du Bienvenue, for more creative cuisine.

🚗 From the d'Ornano car park and bus station in Bayeux, follow the Circuit de Vieux Bayeux trail, with clear descriptions in English and French at every point of interest.

- Map D3
- Office du Tourisme: pont St-Jean. 02 31 51 28 28
- Centre Guillaume-le-Conquérant: rue de Nesmond. 02 31 51 25 50. Open May–Aug: 9am–7pm; mid-Mar–May, Sep–Nov: 9am–6:30pm; Nov–mid-Mar 9:30am–12.30pm, 2–6pm. Closed second week of Jan. Admission €7.80; concessions €3.80; children under 10 free

Top 10 Highlights of Centre Guillaume-le-Conquérant

1. The Tapestry
2. The England of William
3. The Tapestry Explained
4. The Film
5. Harold's Mission to Normandy
6. Harold's Oath
7. Harold's Perjury
8. William Invades England
9. The Battle of Hastings
10. The Death of Harold

1 The Tapestry
The Tapestry itself is displayed completely unfurled in a horseshoe-shaped gallery *(below)*, with dim lighting to preserve its colours. The audio guide walks you through each scene, adding details about the lifestyle of the period.

2 The England of William
Using life-size figures, maps and scale models (including a delightful model of the village of East Meon in Hampshire, England), William's influence on every sphere of English life after his conquest is cleverly portrayed.

3 The Tapestry Explained
A slide show projected onto billowing "sails" describes the Viking invasions of western Europe. Next, echoing the Tapestry, an 85 m (280 ft) band of cloth explains the story told by the embroidery.

4 The Film
Maps and drawings depict the events of the Norman Conquest, and a 14-minute film tells the story from the point of view of William's half-brother Bishop Odo.

5 Harold's Mission to Normandy

In the first scene *(left)*, Edward the Confessor is seen sending Harold from England to Normandy to tell Duke William that he will succeed to the English throne. Harold starts for the coast, preceded by his pack of hounds.

6 Harold's Oath

This critical scene (No 27) provides the moral impetus for the story, told from the Norman point of view: Harold, touching holy relics, swears allegiance to Duke William *(below)*.

7 Harold's Perjury

Harold returns to England from Normandy. On the death of Edward the Confessor, he is crowned king, breaking his oath to William. The appearance of Halley's Comet *(central image)* foretells doom (No 32).

8 William Invades England

As soon as William has ordered his invasion fleet to be built (No 35) *(left)*, the stylized trees that served to break the scenes cease to appear, and the story begins to gather pace.

9 The Battle of Hastings

The battle scenes are marvellously depicted, – full of the clash, clamour and horror of war (Nos 51–58).

10 The Death of Harold

The Tapestry comes to an abrupt end with the death of Harold *(left)* – shot in the eye by an arrow – and the victory of William over the English.

Museum Guide

A visit to the Tapestry itself takes just 20 minutes using the brief but excellent audio guide. It's therefore advisable to take the tour which starts on the first floor and leads up to the Tapestry. A full visit can easily take over two hours. Your ticket also entitles entry to the Musée Baron Gérard (see p14).

Left **Conservatoire de la Dentelle** Right **Jardin Public**

Sights in Bayeux

1 Centre Guillaume-le-Conquérant

Known in France as *La Tapisserie de la Reine Mathilde*, the world-famous Bayeux Tapestry, housed in an impressive 18th-century building, is responsible for one third of this prosperous town's income *(see pp13–14)*.

2 Cathédrale Notre-Dame

Much altered over the centuries, the cathedral was consecrated in the presence of William the Conqueror in 1077.

3 Musée Mémorial de la Bataille de Normandie

Bayeux is the perfect base for visits to the D-Day beaches. This museum provides an excellent introduction for all the family to the Battle of Normandy, told chronologically *(see p30)*.

4 The River Aure

The banks of the River Aure supported many trades in the Middle Ages, including millers, tanners and dyers. The river path offers glimpses of this prosperous era, along with other scenic views, and passes through parks and children's play areas.

5 Conservatoire de la Dentelle

Watch a group of dedicated craftswomen at work as they continue the tradition of intricate Bayeux lacemaking. ◈ *Maison Adam et Eve, 2 rue Bienvenu • Open 10am–12:30pm, 2–6pm Mon–Sat • Free*

6 Le P'tit Train

Discover the history and monuments of Vieux Bayeux during a 35-minute trip aboard the Little Train. ◈ *Departs from the cathedral and the tourist office • 02 97 56 67 46 • Apr–Sep: several times daily • Adm charge*

7 Jardin Public de Bayeux

The botanical garden has a magnificent weeping beech tree 40 ft (13 m) in diameter. ◈ *55 route de Port-en-Bessin • Open Apr–Nov: 9am–8pm daily; Sep–Apr: 9am–5pm daily*

8 Circuit du Vieux Bayeux

Follow the waymarked route round the streets of Vieux Bayeux, with information in English and French at places of interest.

9 British Cemetery and Memorial

The largest British war cemetery in Normandy has 4,144 graves.

10 Old Bayeux

Get a map from the tourist office and discover Old Bayeux through 21 information terminals.

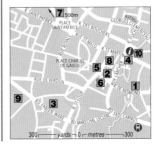

For more on D-Day and the Battle of Normandy See pp28–31

Top 10 Events in William's Life

1. Born in Falaise (1027)
2. Receives the Duchy of Normandy on his father's death (1035)
3. Helped by King Henri I of France, crushes rebel barons in Normandy (1047)
4. Edward the Confessor, his cousin, purportedly promises him the English throne (1051)
5. Harold Godwinson – rival heir to the English throne – swears allegiance to William, perhaps through trickery or under duress (1064)
6. Harold succeeds Edward as king of England (1066)
7. William invades England, defeats Harold, and is crowned at Westminster Abbey on Christmas Day (1066)
8. Ruthlessly crushes all rebellions until England is conquered and united (1072)
9. Commissions the Domesday Book, an invaluable survey of land ownership (1086)
10. Dies in Rouen from a battle wound (1087)

William the Conqueror

A warrior through and through, William, Duke of Normandy and King of England, lived and died by the sword. Yet despite his appetite for battle (the Bayeux Tapestry illustrates some of his forays in Normandy), he had a statesmanlike ability to create order out of chaos. Having won the crown, he made radical changes and improvements to English society by fusing continental practices with native customs – in particular, instituting a type of feudalism that strengthened the monarchy, restrained the power of the church, and supported the educational system of the day. With his wife Matilda, he founded some 30 abbeys, including the two at Caen (see p24).

William the Conqueror

Domesday Book
The Domesday Book, a huge and detailed record of English land ownership at the close of the 11th century, set the seal on Norman land reforms – and the occupation. It is now regarded as one of the most important documents in English history.

For Conqueror connections at Caen and Falaise **See pp24–5, 88**

Top 10 Honfleur

Seductively pretty, with cobbled streets and half-timbered or slate-fronted houses, Honfleur is a working port with a long maritime history. First mentioned in documents of the 11th century, by the 15th it had become a significant fortified port. Its heyday came some 200 years later, when it spawned intrepid explorers like Samuel de Champlain, who set out from here to found Québec. Le Vieux Bassin, the charming old dock at the heart of the town, is brimming with colourful sailing boats; artists have flocked here since the 19th century.

Honfleur artist

⭐ In summer, pick one of the pavement cafés in Le Vieux Bassin.

🚶 Take a tour organized by the tourist office (English tours start 3pm Wed, May–mid-Oct; €6).

- Map F3
- Office du Tourisme: quai Lepaulmier. 02 31 89 23 30
- Musée Eugène Boudin: pl Erik Satie. Open mid-Mar–Sep: 10am–noon, 2–6pm Wed–Mon; Oct–Dec, mid-Feb–mid-Mar: 2:30–5pm Mon, Wed–Fri, 10am–noon, 2:30–5pm Sat–Sun. Adm charge
- Musée de la Marine/ Musée d'Ethnographie: quai St-Etienne. Open mid-Feb–Mar, Oct–mid-Nov: 2:30–5:30pm Tue–Fri, 10am–noon, 2:30–5:30pm Sat–Sun; Apr–Jun, Sep: 10am–noon, 2–6pm Tue–Sun; Jul–Aug: 10am–1pm, 2–6:30pm Tue–Sun. Adm charge
- Les Maisons Satie: 67 blvd Charles V. Open Wed–Mon. Adm charge

Top 10 Sights

1. Le Vieux Bassin
2. Musée Eugène Boudin
3. Église Ste-Catherine
4. Greniers à Sel
5. Église St-Léonard
6. Musée de la Marine
7. Musée d'Ethnographie
8. Les Maisons Satie
9. Chapelle Notre-Dame de Grâce
10. Pont de Normandie

Musée Eugène Boudin

Now housing an exciting collection of 19th- and 20th-century art, the museum *(above)* was founded in 1868 by Honfleur's best-known artists, Boudin and Dubourg.

Église Ste-Catherine

Built to replace a church destroyed in the Hundred Years' War, the largest wooden church in France *(right)* is half-timbered inside and out, with twin naves and tall oak pillars. The heavy bells required a separate stone bell tower.

Le Vieux Bassin

This picturesque harbour *(below)* was built in the 17th century at the behest of Colbert, Louis XIV's chief finance minister, who also ordered the demolition of the ramparts. Quai Ste-Catherine is particularly attractive.

Greniers à Sel

Larger cod catches in the late 16th century increased the demand for salt as a preservative. To accommodate this, two huge salt stores were built in the main street of the *enclos*, the walled town. Stone from the old ramparts was used for the walls, and oak for the roofs – which are still in superb condition. Now they are used for meetings, exhibitions and concerts.

Église St-Léonard
5 From its 16th-century Flamboyant door to its 18th-century octagonal bell tower, St-Léonard *(above)* is a hotchpotch of styles. The copper lectern comes from Villedieu-les-Poêles *(see p99)*.

Musée de la Marine
6 Housed in a 14th-century church, the Musée de la Marine traces the history of the port through scale models, instruments, engravings, cutlasses, cannons and other fascinating artifacts.

Musée d'Ethnographie
7 Nine rooms crammed with objects, furniture and costumes transport you back through the centuries. The most delightful part is the haberdasher's shop, complete down to the ribbon samples.

Les Maisons Satie
8 A suitably offbeat tribute to the eccentric composer Erik Satie, born here in 1866. Videos, surreal room sets and life-size electronic sculptures recreate his fantasy world *(above)*.

Chapelle Notre-Dame de Grâce
9 Explorers came to this enchanting little chapel *(left)* to pray before setting sail. Built in the early 17th century to replace a chapel that fell into the sea, it remains a place of pilgrimage.

Honfleur Artists
Turner, Corot, Courbet, Daubigny, Dubourg, Jongkind, Monet and the Impressionists, the Fauves, Dufy, Friesz, Boudin – these and countless others were drawn to Honfleur by the special quality of light in the Seine estuary, the unspoilt medieval town, and the beauty of the surrounding countryside – the same reasons that Honfleur has a thriving artists' colony today.

Pont de Normandie
10 Opened in 1995, this elegant space-age bridge *(right)* links Honfleur and Le Havre. Its 856 m (2,800 ft) span held the record – albeit briefly – for the world's longest cable-stayed bridge.

Normandy's Top 10

For more on artists in Normandy See pp48–9

🔟 Abbaye de Jumièges

The hauntingly beautiful, bleached white ruins of this Benedictine abbey stand in a loop of the Seine. Founded by St Philibert in 654, following the donation of the estate to him by Queen Bathilde, wife of Clovis II, it was one of a number of abbeys built under the dukes of Normandy as the region turned to Christianity. Despite its chequered history (sacked by Vikings, it was rebuilt only to later be reduced to ruins and used as a quarry), it is a part of Normandy's rich heritage and an important stop on the famous Abbey Route.

Église St-Pierre

🚕 For convenience, try Auberge des Ruines (pl de la Mairie) opposite the abbey entrance; for setting, Auberge du Bac (2 rue Alphonse Callais).

🕐 Explore the magically illuminated abbey on one of the *promenades nocturnes* held on some Saturday nights in July and August. Phone for details.

• 24 rue Guillaume-le-Conquérant, 76480 Jumièges
• Map H3
• 02 35 37 24 02
• www.monum.fr
• Open mid-Apr–mid-Sep: 9:30am–6:30pm daily; mid-Sep–mid-Apr and Easter: 9:30am–1pm, 2:30–5:30pm. Closed 1 Jan, 1 May, 1 Nov, 11 Nov, 25 Dec
• Admission: adults €5; 18- to 25-year-olds €3.50; children under 18 free. Nov–Mar: first Sun of the month free

Top 10 Features
1. West Façade
2. Storeroom
3. Nave
4. Transept
5. Choir
6. Charles VII's Passage
7. Église St-Pierre
8. Chapterhouse
9. Cloister
10. Abbey Dwelling-house

1 West Façade
Stark and simple, the church of Notre-Dame's impressive Romanesque façade was built around 1060, with a projecting porch flanked by two massive towers. Square at the base, octagonal above, they originally had wooden spires.

2 Storeroom
Once a welcoming hall for important guests, the storeroom, Gothic in design, Romanesque in decoration, is intact but for its ribbed vaulting.

3 Nave
Only the walls of Normandy's tallest Romanesque nave *(left)* still stand, left open to the skies after the demolition of the plaster vault that replaced the original, wood ceiling.

4 Transept
The west wall is all that survives of the 11th-century transept. The transept crossing was topped by a lantern tower, to let in maximum light in poor weather.

5 Choir

Nothing remains of the earliest choir. The ruins *(left)* are from a 13th-century Gothic version, comprising an ambulatory with seven radiating chapels. An ornate rood screen is decorated with bas-reliefs illustrating the passion of Christ.

10 *in Abbey grounds*

7 Église St-Pierre

The western section of this church was probably built in the first few decades of the 9th century, predating the Viking raids on Jumièges. It is an important monument of the Carolingian period.

6 Charles VII's Passage

This covered arcade, built in the early 1330s to link the two churches, predates Charles VII, but was named after a visit he made here with his mistress, Agnès Sorel, whose heart is buried under a marble slab in the north transept chapel.

8 Chapterhouse

It was in this 11th- to 12th-century hall that a chapter from the rules of St Benedict was read out every morning, and monastic affairs were discussed. Between the 12th and mid-13th centuries, it became the abbots' burial ground.

9 Cloister

Today, the cloister is an expanse of grass with a yew tree at its centre, but it was once the heart of the abbey, used by monks for promenades, ceremonies, meditation and processions.

10 Abbey Dwelling-house

This imposing house *(left)* was built for François de Harlay de Champvallon – a "commendatory" abbot appointed directly by the king.

The Maurists

After a period of spiritual decline in the 16th and 17th centuries, the Maurists, a fiercely intellectual and devout congregation of St Maur founded in Paris in 1618, were dispatched to reform Jumièges Abbey. Among their improvements to its physical structure were a vast library, the abbey dwelling-house, and a monumental double staircase leading to a broad terrace and the gardens beyond.

For more on the Abbey Route **See p76**

19

Cathédrale Notre-Dame, Rouen

In the historic heart of the city, this magnificent cathedral took nearly 400 years to build. It stands as a record of the entire span of French Gothic archi-tecture. Through the centuries, it has captured the imagination of artists, most famously Monet, who was so obsessed with the west façade that he painted it 30 times between 1892 and 1894 – at different times of day and year, and in various weather conditions, in order to capture the subtle changes of colour and light. His thick impasto suggests the texture of the ornately carved stone.

Spire of the Cathédrale Notre-Dame

🍰 In a half-timbered building on a charming old street opposite the cathedral's north front, Dame Cakes (70 rue St-Romain) has a wonderful selection of tarts and gâteaux.

👁 You can get a good view of the famous west façade from the tourist office (25 pl de la Cathédrale). Albane Courtyard (currently closed for refurbish-ment) on the north side is where relics of earlier cathedrals have been discovered.

• pl de la Cathédrale, 76000 Rouen
• Map M6
• 02 35 71 51 23
• Open Apr–Oct: 9am–7pm daily; Nov–Mar: 9am–noon, 2–6pm daily. Closed Mon am
• Free
• Guided tours on public holidays

Top 10 Features

1. West Façade
2. Spire
3. Booksellers' Courtyard
4. Nave
5. Lantern Tower
6. Choir
7. Lady Chapel
8. Ambulatory Tombs
9. Library Staircase
10. Window of St Julian the Hospitaller

1 West Façade
Familiar through Monet's paintings, this richly sculpted façade *(right)* reflects the evolu-tion of the Gothic style. The most elaborate part is Roulland le Roux's early 16th-century central porch.

2 Spire
Flaubert was famously rude about it, but the people of Rouen have grown fond of this cast-iron spire, the tallest in France. A bold 19th-century design, it matches the height of the hills that surround the city.

3 Booksellers' Courtyard
Created as a short cut for the local canons, this narrow courtyard is notable for the intricacy of its carvings.

4 Nave
Typical of the early Gothic style, the exquisitely proportioned nave *(left)* has four storeys: arches, tribunes (in this case, false ones), gallery and upper windows.

Lantern Tower

5 The lantern tower *(left)* rises a breathtaking 151 m (495 ft) above the transept crossing from floor to keystone, flooding the interior with light. At the base of each of its columns, busts 1 m (3 ft) high, said to represent the tower's builders, appear to be shouldering its weight.

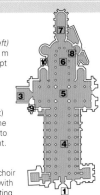

Choir

6 The fine 13th-century choir is half-circled by tall pillars with vast carved capitals supporting pointed arches. The choir stalls, from the same period, are carved with comic scenes.

Lady Chapel

7 The delicate 14th-century Lady Chapel contains the tombs of more than 150 dignitaries, including that of the Cardinals of Amboise by le Roux.

Ambulatory Tombs

8 Here are effigies of Rollo *(above)*, William Long Sword (known for his short stature rather than the length of his sword), and Richard the Lionheart, who ordered that his heart be buried here *(see p41)*.

Library Staircase

9 The lower two flights of this superb staircase *(above)* are the work of Guillaume Pontifs, while the upper two are 18th-century copies. The ogee arch above the wrought-iron door is typically Flamboyant Gothic.

Window of St Julian the Hospitaller

10 In jewel-like blues and reds, this early 13th-century stained-glass window *(right)* tells the tragic story of St Julian, who accidentally murdered his parents and founded a hospital in penance.

The History of the Cathedral

Building started in the mid-12th century on the site of two earlier cathedrals: the first, 4th-century; the second, an 11th-century Romanesque building from which the crypt survives. After a fire in 1200, work continued on the present building into the 16th century. Having survived the next four centuries more or less intact, it was devastated by bombing on 19 April 1944; only two flying buttresses prevented the whole building from collapsing. Repairs continue to the present day.

For more on Norman Abbeys **See pp46–7**

Left **Aître St-Maclou, detail** Right **Église Jeanne d'Arc**

🔟 Other Sights in Rouen

1 Musée des Beaux-Arts
Highlights include paintings by Caravaggio, Velásquez, Monet, Géricault, Dufy and Modigliani. 🕙 *espl Marcel Duchamp • Map M5 • Open 10am–6pm Wed–Mon • Adm charge*

2 Aître St-Maclou
This tranquil 14th-century courtyard was a plague cemetery. The timbered galleries are decorated with *memento mori*. 🕙 *186 rue Martainville (at end of passage) • Map N6 • Open 9am–6pm daily • Free*

3 Église St-Maclou
A masterpiece of Flamboyant Gothic. 🕙 *Map N6 • Open 10am–5pm Mon & Fri, 3–5:30pm Sun • Free*

4 Gros Horloge
Moved from the Gothic belfry to a purpose-built arch in 1527, the Great Clock has two dials, a single hour hand and a panel showing the phases of the moon. 🕙 *191 rue du Gros Horloge • Open Tue–Sun • Map L5*

Gros Horloge

5 Palais de Justice
A magnificent example of late-medieval architecture, despite a 19th-century wing. 🕙 *36 rue aux Juifs • Map M5 • Closed to the public*

6 Église Jeanne d'Arc
The cross outside this striking modern church marks the site of Joan's martyrdom. 🕙 *pl du Vieux Marché • Map L5 • Open 10am–noon, 2–6pm Mon–Thu & Sat, 2–6pm Fri & Sun*

7 Musée National de l'Éducation
Charts 500 years of children's education. 🕙 *185 rue Eau-de-Robec • Map N5 • Open 10am–noon, 2–6pm Mon, Wed–Fri, 2–6pm Sat, Sun and school hols • Adm charge*

8 Abbatiale St-Ouen
The Cavaillé-Coll organ at this Flamboyant abbey is world-famous. 🕙 *rue des Faulx • Map N5 • Open Apr–Oct: 10am–noon, 2–6pm; Nov–Mar: 10am–noon, 2–5pm. Closed Mon & Fri • Free*

9 Musée Le Secq des Tournelles
The world's largest collection of historic wrought-ironware. 🕙 *2 rue Jacques Villon • Map M5 • Open 10am–1pm, 2–6pm Wed–Mon • Adm charge*

10 Musée de la Céramique
Charts the evolution of Rouen's earthenware. 🕙 *Hotel d'Hôcqueville, 1 rue Faucon • Map M4 • Open 10am–1pm, 2–6pm Wed–Mon • Adm charge*

For Rouen's wonderful Jardin des Plantes **See p44**
Buy a carte-musée at the tourist office for discounts to sites

Joan of Arc

Although the facts of Joan's life are well recorded, she remains an enigma. The Maid of Orléans, as she came to be known, was from a pious peasant family, could barely read or write, yet succeeded in persuading the Dauphin to let her lead his army. The image of the androgynous, armour-clad Joan is iconic, portrayed through the centuries by sculptors, painters, playwrights and film-makers. She clearly had conviction and charisma, but did the "voices" she heard throughout her short life make her a visionary or a schizophrenic? After her canonization, France adopted Joan as her patron saint, whose feast day (30 May) is celebrated throughout the country.

Execution in Rouen

Joan of Arc's execution was originally to take place on 24 May 1431, but at the last moment she broke down and recanted. She later retracted that recantation, and met her fate on 30 May.

Top 10 Events of Joan of Arc's Life

1. Born in Domrémy on 6 January 1412
2. Aged 13, hears voices for the first time
3. Four years later, the voices tell her to save France from the English
4. Gains an audience with Dauphin Charles on 9 March 1429
5. Leads the French to victory at Orléans (8 May); Charles' coronation follows (17 July)
6. Captured by the Burgundians in May 1430; they sell her to the English
7. Tried in Rouen for heresy and witchcraft, 21 February to 23 May 1431
8. Burned at the stake in pl du Vieux Marché on 30 May 1431
9. Rehabilitated in 1456
10. Canonized in 1920

Joan of Arc welcomed to Loches by Charles VII

🔟 Caen

The capital of Basse-Normandie, Caen is a lively, cultured university town with a compact historic centre. Although devastated in 1944, it was carefully restored, and today successfully blends modern with old, dominated still by William the Conqueror's Château Ducal and his two great abbeys. The presence of a colourful marina in the heart of the town is a reminder that Caen is also a proud seaport. Equidistant from Cherbourg, Mont-St-Michel and Rouen, it makes an excellent base for exploring Normandy.

Abbaye-aux-Hommes, façade

🍴 There's a wide range of eateries in the Quartier Vaugueux.

🚗 Park at the Côte de Nacre car park north of the city for just €2.50 per day; then travel by tram (€1.50) to the city centre.

• Map D3
• Office de Tourisme: pl St-Pierre. Map M2. 02 31 27 14 14
• Abbaye-aux-Hommes: Map L2. Guided tours in French at 9:30am, 11am, 2:30pm, 4pm daily. Admission €3
• Abbey-aux-Dames: Map N1. Guided tours 2:30 & 4pm daily. Free
• Musée des Beaux-Arts: Map M1. Open 9:30am–6pm Wed–Mon. Admission €3
• Musée de Normandie: Map M1. Open 9:30am–6pm Wed–Mon. Admission €3
• Le Mémorial de Caen: Map L1. 02 31 06 06 45. www.memorial-caen.fr Open 9am–7pm Tue–Sun. Closed 25 Dec–31 Jan. Admission €18

Top 10 Sights

1. Abbaye-aux-Hommes
2. Abbaye-aux-Dames
3. Château Ducal
4. Musée des Beaux-Arts
5. Musée de Normandie
6. Le Mémorial de Caen
7. Église St-Pierre
8. Rue St-Pierre
9. Marina
10. Quartier Vaugueux

1 Abbaye-aux-Hommes

William and Matilda were cousins; at first, the pope opposed their marriage. He relented, and they atoned by each founding an abbey: in William's case, the Abbaye-aux-Hommes (see pp46, 87).

2 Abbaye-aux-Dames

Matilda's tomb is marked by a slab of black marble in the choir of her abbey church, La Trinité. Her beautiful abbey (below), in creamy Caen stone, is now the Regional Council headquarters.

3 Château Ducal

Built as a royal home, William's hilltop castle became a fortress in 1204. The ramparts (above), Chapelle St-Georges and the great hall of Henri I's palace are all that remain.

4 Musée des Beaux-Arts

Within the castle walls is this wide-ranging fine-art collection, strong on 17th-century French and Italian painting (see p53).

For more on William the Conqueror See p15

5 Musée de Normandie
Also in the Château complex, this museum presents a survey of Norman life, with exhibits ranging from the prehistoric to the industrial *(left)*.

6 Le Mémorial de Caen
Northwest of the city, this major museum of remembrance and peace traces the causes and consequences of World War II and the Cold War *(see p52)*.

7 Église St-Pierre
The church is notable for its impressively ornate Renaissance apse and its much-copied spire *(above)*, rebuilt after 1944.

8 Rue St-Pierre
This lively shopping street *(below)* is lined with historic buildings. Turn down rue Froide, full of interesting shops and hidden alleys, then left to reach place St-Sauveur, scene of a Friday market since 1026 *(see p58)*.

9 Marina
Tour Leroy stands at the entrance to the old harbour. Today, a yacht marina *(above)*, picturesque in summer, marks the canal that leads to the ferry port of Ouistreham.

10 Quartier Vaugueux
This is Caen's "petit Montmartre" *(below)*, with a jumble of pretty buildings, old street-lights, and a great mix of restaurants and cafés.

Caen Orientation
The city grew up around William's Château Ducal, flanked by the two abbeys to east and west, with all the other sights of interest (except the Mémorial) between. Buses and trams arrive close to the Église St-Pierre and the tourist office, which occupies a fine mansion, Hôtel d'Escoville (don't miss its Renaissance courtyard to the left of the entrance).

For nearby wartime sights **See pp28–31**

Deauville and La Côte Fleurie

Between Honfleur and Cabourg, the Norman coastline becomes a playground: resorts, casinos, watersports, sunshine, sandy beaches backed by wooded hills. It all started in Trouville, which triggered the 19th-century rage for sea bathing. Next comes racy, romantic Deauville – created in the 1860s by a trio of wealthy entrepreneurs, embellished in 1910 with boardwalk, casino and racecourse. In contrast, Touques and Dives-sur-Mer have historic links with William the Conqueror, while stately Cabourg is forever associated with Marcel Proust.

Trouville market

In Deauville, Bar du Soleil and Bar de la Mer on Les Planches are great for people-watching. If you are looking for regional specialities, try Café de Paris in the central square.

In Trouville, eat *moules-frites* at one of the many water-front restaurants, such as Les Vapeurs.

Dress up to visit Deauville: it will make you feel the part.

Access to Deauville beach is free; its gaily coloured parasols – folded in a way unique to the town – are, however, quite expensive to hire.

- Map E3
- Office du Tourisme: pl de la Mairie, Deauville. 02 31 14 40 00
- Office du Tourisme: Jardin de l'Hôtel de Ville, Cabourg. 02 31 91 20 00

Top 10 Sights

1. Deauville
2. Trouville-sur-Mer
3. Touques
4. Manoir des Evêques
5. Villerville
6. Mont Canisy
7. Falaise des Vaches Noires
8. Houlgate
9. Dives-sur-Mer
10. Cabourg

Deauville

Racehorses pounding the beach at sunrise, a glamorous wooden boardwalk, the glittering casino, the sumptuous Hôtel Normandy, the Bar du Soleil, the Pompeian Baths, designer shops, marinas, racecourses, extravagant mock-Tudor villas – a glossy picture.

Trouville-sur-Mer

In contrast to its neighbour Deauville, Trouville exudes a terrific, happy-go-lucky air – due in part to its south-facing waterfront boulevard, trawlers and fish market, aquarium, children's amusements and wonderfully florid 1912 casino and town hall.

Touques

The vestiges of William the Conqueror's castle can be visited at Bonneville, above his port of Touques. In the neat town centre stands the 11th-century church of St-Pierre *(left)*.

4 Manoir des Evêques
Dip your toes into the beautiful Pays d'Auge *(see pp32–3)* with a visit to Canapville's half-timbered Manoir des Evêques, one of its loveliest buildings.

5 Villerville
In the summer months, this seaside town *(right)* surrounded by woods and meadows organizes long nature walks along the coast.

6 Mont Canisy
Mont Canisy rises above Deauville, with views from Le Havre to the Orne; underground is a warren of German bunkers and tunnels.

7 Falaise des Vaches Noires
A walk at low tide between Villers and Houlgate takes you past the "cliff of the black cows", rich in fossils.

8 Houlgate
Like Villers-sur-Mer, Houlgate is a family resort notable for its Neo-Norman architecture, all half-timbering, gables, turrets and towers.

9 Dives-sur-Mer
The former port from which William set sail to conquer England boasts a magnificent oak-framed market hall *(see p58)* and the church of Notre-Dame *(right)*, founded in 1067.

10 Cabourg
Take tea at the Grand Hôtel *(below)*, so vividly described by Proust in *A la recherche du temps perdu* and, like Cabourg itself, still redolent of those genteel 19th-century days.

The High Life

A non-stop round of film festivals, horse racing, yachting regattas, tennis and golf tournaments, international bridge championships, jazz, and vintage car rallies keeps Deauville buzzing all year. But it's the hectic 100-day summer season that brings the beautiful people out in force, staying at the Normandy, dining at Ciro's, shopping for Cartier, posing on Les Planches, gambling, racegoing, or sipping cocktails on their yachts. Elegant, snooty, monied, and not a little flashy: that's Deauville.

🔟 D-Day Beaches

On 6 June 1944, Nazi-occupied France was invaded by British, American, Commonwealth and Canadian troops, resulting in the country's liberation. The Allied landings on the beaches of the Seine Bay (still known by their wartime codenames) and the ferocious Battle of Normandy that followed are commemorated today through a moving mixture of museums, memorials and cemeteries. Beautifully maintained and presented with great clarity, they give visitors a fascinating insight into the events of that momentous summer.

Arromanches beach, site of the British landing

🍴 Three seaside restaurants recommended for their seafood: La Marine at Arromanches, Le Bistrot d'à Côté at Port-en-Bessin and La Marée at Grandcamp-Maisy.

✪ Decide in advance which of the many museums, memorials and beaches you most want to see. Consider starting at the Musée de la Bataille de Normandie in Bayeux and ending at Arromanches 360 (see p30).

• Map C3, D3
• Office du Tourisme: pont St-Jean, Bayeux. 02 31 51 28 28
• Observation bunker, La Pointe du Hoc: Open 10am–5pm daily. Free.

Top 10 D-Day Highlights

1 Utah Beach and Ste-Mère-Eglise
2 La Pointe du Hoc
3 Omaha Beach
4 American Cemetery
5 Batteries de Longues
6 Arromanches
7 Gold Beach
8 Juno Beach
9 Sword Beach
10 Pegasus Bridge

1 Utah Beach and Ste-Mère-Eglise
Over 13,000 US para-troops were dropped into the Cotentin marshland; the US 4th Division came ashore on Utah *(above)* and linked up with them.

2 La Pointe du Hoc
Preserved as it was at the end of fighting, this bleak headland *(below)* was stormed by elite US Rangers using ropes and ladders to scale the cliff, with heavy casualties.

3 Omaha Beach
"Bloody Omaha" *(above)* saw terrible losses among the 1st and 29th US Divisions. A viewing table, two museums, 11 monu-ments and the American Cemetery tell the story.

4 American Cemetery
Formal yet serene, the American Cemetery *(main image)*, containing 9,386 graves, receives many thousands of visitors each year. ✪ Colleville-sur-Mer

Batteries de Longues

Near Arromanches, this is the only German battery still to have its guns. Its observation post, on the edge of the cliff, can also be visited. ◈ *Longues-sur-Mer*

Arromanches

The remains of the artificial Mulberry Harbour make a startling sight *(above)* – a testament to the ingenuity of Winston Churchill, who realized that if the troops wanted to land, they would have to bring their harbours with them.

Gold Beach

Soon after they landed here, the British 50th Division took Arromanches, enabling the Mulberry Harbour to be put in place.

Juno Beach

Several small seaside resorts line the beach assigned to the 3rd Canadian Division. A huge cross of Lorraine *(above)* commemorates the triumphant return of General de Gaulle, who landed here on 14 June.

Sword Beach

Though the Allies established the beachhead with relative ease, the vital objective of Caen was thwarted, and the inhabitants had to wait another 34 days for their city to be liberated.

Pegasus Bridge

The first Allies to land in France were the men of the British 6th Airborne Division, who seized this strategic bridge *(below)*, renamed after their insignia. ◈ *Bénouville/Ranville*

Touring the Beaches

Drivers can follow two themed and signposted routes, "Overlord–L'Assaut" and "D-Day–Le Choc", which are backed up by information "totems" at each place of interest (look for the dove symbol). The accompanying booklet (including a total of eight routes around Normandy), *The D-Day Landings and Battle of Normandy*, is available from local tourist offices, where you will also find details of recommended bus and taxi tour operators.

Left **Musée Airborne** Right **Arromanches 360**

🔟 D-Day Museums

1 Musée Mémorial de la Bataille de Normandie
A good place to start, this museum gives an excellent overview of the 77-day battle. ◈ blvd Fabian-Ware, Bayeux • Map D3 • 02 31 51 46 90 • Open daily • Adm charge

2 Musée de la Liberté
An absorbing "museum without weapons", describing life in occupied France and the liberation of the Cotentin Peninsula. ◈ Quinéville • Map B2 • Open mid-Mar–mid-Nov: daily • Adm charge

3 Musée Airborne
Shaped like a parachute, this museum commemorates the American paratroops dropped behind Utah Beach. ◈ Ste-Mère-Eglise • Map B3 • Open Feb–Nov: Tue–Sun • Adm charge

4 Musée des Rangers
The museum tells the saga of the US Rangers, from their formation in June 1942 to their heroic assault on Pointe du Hoc. ◈ Grandcamp-Maisy • Map C3 • 02 31 92 33 51 • Call for opening times

Bill Millin's bagpipes, Musée Mémorial Pegasus

Musée des Épaves

5 Musée des Épaves
A fascinating collection of D-Day wrecks. ◈ rte de Bayeux, Port-en-Bessin • Map C3 • 02 31 21 17 06 • Open Jun–Sep: daily; May: 10am–noon, 2–6pm Sat & Sun • Adm charge

6 Musée du Débarquement
Port Winston, the artificial harbour constructed in the bay outside, is brought vividly to life. ◈ St-Côme, Arromanches • Map D3 • Open Feb–Dec: daily • Adm charge

7 Arromanches 360
Witness the events of D-Day in an 18-minute film, The Price of Freedom. ◈ St-Côme, Arromanches • Map D3 • Open Feb–Dec: daily • Adm charge

8 Juno Beach Centre
A museum depicting the Canadian contribution to D-Day. ◈ Courseulles-sur-Mer • Map D3 • Open Feb–Dec: daily • Adm charge

9 Musée Mémorial Pégasus
Bill Millin's bagpipes are among the exhibits commemorating the British glider assault at Bénouville. ◈ Ranville-Bénouville • Map E3, D3 • Open Feb–Dec: daily • Adm charge

10 Musée de la Batterie de Merville
The sound-and-light show and a Douglas C-47 plane are worth a visit. ◈ Merville Franceville • Map D3 • Open 15 Mar–15 Nov: daily; rest of the year: by appt • Adm charge

For information on the peace museum, Le Mémorial **See pp25, 52**

Top 10 Amazing D-Day Statistics

1. 4,000 ships in the fleet
2. 5,800 bomber planes
3. 4,900 fighter planes
4. 153,000 troops
5. 20,000 vehicles
6. 11,000 casualties
7. 2,500 dead
8. 2,052,299 men came ashore following D-Day
9. 3,098,259 tons of stores
10. 640,000 Germans killed, wounded or taken prisoner in the Battle of Normandy

D-Day landing

Operation Overlord

The planning, manufacture of armaments, and training of men for the epic Allied invasion of Normandy in June 1944, code-named Operation Overlord, began in earnest in the winter of 1943, led by Generals Eisenhower and Montgomery. D-Day was planned for 5 June, but was delayed for 24 hours due to bad weather. The unfavourable conditions, and an expected attack elsewhere (on Pas-de-Calais, nearer to Britain), caught the Germans by surprise when dawn brought the vast Allied fleet to the sandy beaches of the Seine Bay, flanked by airborne forces to east and west. "It was as if every ship and every plane that had ever been built was there," said one British soldier. "The beach was alive with the shambles and the order of war … there were dead men and wounded men and men brewing tea." Once beachheads were established on Utah, Omaha, Gold, Juno and Sword Beaches, initial penetration into Normandy was uneven. Cherbourg fell on 26 June, Caen not until 9 July. Fighting conditions were grim amongst the hedgerows of the Bocage (see p98), and it was not until 21 August, after the Germans were cornered in a pincer movement in the Battle of the Falaise-Mortain Pocket, that the Battle of Normandy was finally won. Paris was liberated on 25 August.

British troops of the 56th Infantry landing on the beaches of Normandy, 6 June 1944

🔟 Pays d'Auge

Orchards of apple and pear, thatched houses and half-timbered manors tucked into the hills, fat brown-and-white cows, immaculate studs, farmhouses selling cider and cheese – that's the Pays d'Auge. Stretching north to the Côte Fleurie (see pp26–7), bisected by the River Touques, the region perfectly encapsulates the distinctive charms of Normandy. The highlights described here are a delightful selection of villages, views, manors, châteaux and abbeys – and, of course, a Camembert museum and a Calvados distillery.

Manoir de Coupesarte

❷ **Beuvron-en-Auge** makes a good place for lunch, with plenty of choice, including the gastronomic Pavé d'Auge *(see p56)*.

❸ **Driven in numerical order, the sights listed here make an excellent circular tour.**

• Map E3–4, F3–4
• Office du Tourisme: 11 rue d'Alençon, Lisieux. 02 31 48 18 10
• Château St-Germain-de-Livet: Map F4. Open Feb–end Sep, mid-Oct–Nov: 11am–6pm Wed–Sun; Jul–Aug: 10am–7pm daily. Adm charge
• Château de Vendeuvre: Map E4. Open May–Sep: 11am–6pm daily. Adm charge
• Château de Crèvecoeur-en-Auge: Map E4. Open Apr–Jun, Sep: 11am–6pm daily; Jul–Aug: 11am–7pm daily; Oct: 11am–6pm Mon–Sat, 2–6pm Sun. Adm charge
• Distillerie Busnel: Map F3. 02 32 57 80 08. Open Apr–Oct daily. Adm charge

Top 10 Highlights

1. Lisieux
2. Château St-Germain-de-Livet
3. Manoir de Coupesarte
4. Vimoutiers
5. St-Pierre-sur-Dives
6. Château de Vendeuvre
7. Château de Crèvecoeur-en-Auge
8. Beuvron-en-Auge
9. Clermont-en-Auge
10. Distillerie Busnel, Cormeilles

❶ Lisieux
The principal town of the region is inextricably linked with Ste Thérèse, who achieved post-humous renown for her book, *Histoire d'une âme* (Story of a Soul), and was canonized in 1925. On her account, hundreds of thousands of pilgrims flock here every year.

❷ Château St-Germain-de-Livet
A visit to this enchanting château feels like entering a private world. Outside, turrets, towers, timbers and cleverly patterned brick; inside, oak furniture, Renaissance frescoes and thick, creaking floorboards.

❸ Manoir de Coupesarte
A short track off the D47 brings you to the most romantic of all the Auge manors *(top left)*. It's privately owned, but you can enter the adjoining farmyard to see the late-15th-century timbered, turreted house.

❹ Vimoutiers
In the centre of Vimoutiers is a statue of Marie Harel *(right)*, credited with inventing Camembert in the sleepy village of that name *(see p110)*. The Musée du Camembert tells the story.

➜ *In Lisieux, you can visit Les Buissonnets, Thérèse's childhood home, as well as the Cathédrale St-Pierre, where she attended mass.*

5 St-Pierre-sur-Dives

The market town huddles round its huge, sheltering church, all that is left of the rich Benedictine abbey that once stood here *(see p92)*. The monks originally constructed the town's venerable market hall *(see p59)*.

6 Château de Vendeuvre

There's plenty to do here: step back into the 18th century in the elegant château itself; visit the museum of miniature furniture *(see p53)*; or wander in the delightful "surprise" water gardens.

7 Château de Crèvecoeur-en-Auge

A rare chance to look inside a medieval lord's moated, fortified Auge manor. The former agricultural buildings house a museum of oil prospecting, connected with the Schlumberger Foundation.

9 Clermont-en-Auge

In the village, look for St-Michel-de-Clermont, a charming chapel offering a fine panorama of the Pays d'Auge and the marshland beyond.

10 Distillerie Busnel, Cormeilles

At this distillery, you can learn about the process of making the cider brandy Calvados – and, of course, taste the results.

8 Beuvron-en-Auge

One of the loveliest and most popular villages in the area. Charming houses, each one striped with old beams and dripping with geraniums *(above)*, cluster around the main square. There is a fine manor house.

The Cider Route

If you like cider, you can do no better than to follow the signposted Route du Cidre, linking the Pays d'Auge's principal cider-making villages – such as delightful Cambremer, Bonnebosq and Beuvron-en-Auge – by pretty backroads. The route also passes about 20 local producers (recognizable by the sign "Cru de Cambremer"), who offer tours of their cellars, and tastings *(see p94)*. Pick up a "Tourist Routes" leaflet at a tourist office.

For recommended cafés and restaurants in this region **See p95**

Fondation Claude Monet, Giverny

Travelling by train between Vernon and Gasny in April 1883, Monet spotted Giverny through the window. It was love at first sight, and he moved here with Alice Hoschedé as swiftly as possible. He planted his garden so that he could paint in every season. He considered it his masterpiece, a painting of dazzling colours created with nature. After his death, the house and gardens fell into disrepair, but between 1977 and 1980 the Académie des Beaux-Arts restored them to their original condition – a living memorial to Monet and his work.

Water Garden

🅞 For refreshment, try Hôtel Baudy (81 rue Claude Monet), or the café of the Musée des Impressionnismes.

✪ Avoid the crowds by visiting early or late in the season.

• 84 rue Claude Monet, 27620 Giverny
• Map K4
• 02 32 51 28 21
• www.fondation-monet.com
• Open Apr–1 Nov: 9:30am–6pm daily
• Admission €9 students and under-12s €5; disabled €4; under-7s free
• Musée des Impressionnismes: 99 rue Claude Monet. 02 32 51 94 65. www.mdig.fr Open 1 May–13 Jul: 10am–6pm daily; 14 Jul–31 Oct: 10am–6pm Tue–Sun (open on bank holiday Mondays). Admission €5.50; children €3. Free on first Sun of each month. Disabled access throughout.

Top 10 Highlights

1. Water Garden
2. Japanese Bridge
3. Clos Normand
4. Pink House
5. Japanese Prints
6. Sitting Room-Studio
7. Monet's Bedroom
8. Dining Room
9. Kitchen
10. Water Lily Studio

Water Garden
Exotic, asymmetrical, Monet's water garden *(above)* is a place for calm contemplation of nature, amongst a gentle riot of plant life: rhododendrons, weeping willows, water lilies and much more.

Japanese Bridge
This famous, wisteria-draped bridge *(below)* reflects Monet's abiding interest in Japanese prints, many of them in the Pink House collection.

Clos Normand
Monet's French-style garden *(below)* is a triumph of symmetry, colour and judicious planting, with flowers in bloom all season.

Pink House
In this charming pink stucco house *(main image)*, Monet entertained Cézanne, Renoir, Matisse and other famous artists of his time, as well as his good friend Georges Clemenceau.

Japanese Prints

Monet's precious woodblock prints are hung in several rooms, according to a plan drawn up by Monet himself.

Sitting Room-Studio

Monet used to come to his simply furnished studio *(left)* after dinner to relax, smoke, and examine his day's work.

Monet's Bedroom

The room where Monet slept for 43 years, and eventually died, still has most of its original furniture, including a fine 18th-century inlaid desk. Endearingly, Monet kept works by the artists he most admired in his bedroom *(below)*: among them Cézanne, Renoir, Manet, Pissarro and Rodin – a collection now scattered worldwide.

Dining Room

Imagine Monet, together with Alice Hoschedé, her children and visiting artists, seated around the large dining table in this perfectly restored room, painted in two shades of yellow, with faïence plates and Japanese prints on the walls, and vestiges of the dinner service in two dressers.

Kitchen

Little seems to have changed over the past century in this delightful room *(above)* – an extension built by Monet, with blue-and-white-tiled walls, a handsome cast-iron range, butler's sink, terracotta floor, and burnished copper pots and pans.

Water Lily Studio

His sight affected by cataracts, Monet built this large, light studio between 1914 and 1916, to work on his water lily series. It now houses the shop of the Fondation Claude Monet.

Sight Guide

From the entrance on rue Claude Monet into an outbuilding, stairs lead down to the water lily studio. Outside is the Clos Normand. In the southwestern corner, an underground passage leads to the water garden and Japanese bridge. On entering the Pink House, beside the entrance, you must turn left and follow the circuit round from the small blue reading room to the sitting room-studio, then upstairs to the bedrooms. The tour ends with the dining room and kitchen.

Normandy's Top 10

For more on artists in Normandy **See pp48–9**

35

Left **The Terra Café** Right **The grounds of the museum**

🔟 Musée des Impressionnismes, Giverny

1 The Museum
The original museum on this site was the Musée d'Art Américain, which was replaced in 2009 by a museum entirely dedicated to the Impressionist movement. The Musée d'Orsay in Paris is the main partner.

2 The Collection
The museum doesn't have a permanent collection; instead, it features temporary exhibitions on the theme of Impressionism.

3 Impressionist Painters
The museum, in the heart of the village of Giverny, explores the artistic impact of the Impressionist movement on the second half of the 20th century. Both world-famous and lesser-known artists are on display.

4 The Building
Terraced into the hillside, with vine-clad roofs, the building was designed by Philippe Robert to blend in with its surroundings. Inside, there are three exhibition galleries and a 200-seat auditorium.

5 Exhibitions
The museum houses about two exhibitions each year, mostly showcasing works on loan from the Musée d'Orsay and private collections.

An exhibition at the Musée des Impressionnismes

6 Museum Gardens
In landscape architect Mark Rudkin's design, beds are simply planted in monochrome colour schemes, divided by hedges. In 2006, the gardens of the museum were awarded the Jardin Remarquable label.

7 The Terra Café
Enjoy quiches, salads, grilled fish and meat and American pies at this elegant café. There is also a tea room, and a terrace in the heart of the garden.

8 The Hills of Giverny
At the back of the museum a large meadow opens out on to a hill filled with poppies, daisies and cornflowers. This is the very landscape that inspired Monet. A walk through this meadow is a good way to immerse yourself in the Impressionist mindset.

9 Guided Tours
Audio tours are available in English and many other languages for both individuals and small groups.

10 Concerts and Events
From April to October, concerts and other events are staged in the auditorium and garden. Consult the website for more details. ◈ www.mdig.fr

Top 10 Events in Monet's Life

1. 1840: born on 14 November in Paris
2. 1858: introduced to painting outside by Eugène Boudin
3. 1866: enjoys first success at the Salon
4. 1870: introduced to art dealer, Paul Durand-Ruel
5. 1871: starts collecting Japanese prints
6. 1874: holds "Impressionist" exhibition with Renoir, Sisley and other artists
7. 1883: discovers Giverny and moves into the Pink House
8. 1892: starts work on the garden and Rouen Cathedral series; marries Alice Hoschedé
9. 1916: starts *Water Lily* series
10. 1926: dies on 6 December at Giverny

Monet and Impressionism

As a child, Monet was encouraged to paint en plein air *(outdoors). He found the established techniques of studio-painting inadequate to his purposes. Fascinated by the illusory effects of sunlight and the weather on his subject, he strived to "capture the moment" with quick, bold brushstrokes, concerned more with effect than with sharp naturalistic detail – a technique that, despite his early success, did not endear him to the Salon. His painting,* Impression, Sunrise, *exhibited in a show with other sympathetic artists, led a critic to coin the term "Impressionism", and he was heralded as the father of the style. His discovery of Giverny coincided with a new energy and confidence in his painting. The colours in his carefully planned gardens provided him with an ever-changing palette, and in the years he spent there, he painted his best-known works. His life had been dogged by financial hardship and tragedy; at Giverny, he was solvent and successful for the first time.*

Claude Monet in his studio at Giverny

Sunrise, Le Havre, 1872

 Following pages **Manoir du Courboyer, Nocé**

Left **Gallic leader Vercingetorix surrenders to Julius Caesar** Right **Battle of Formigny**

Moments in History

1 58–51 BC: Roman Invasion
By 56 BC the Romans had swept through the region, conquering the Celtic Gallic settlers. They built roads, amphitheatres, viaducts and major fortified settlements, including Rotomagus (Rouen), Augustodurum (Bayeux) and Mediolanum (Evreux).

2 911: Treaty of St-Clair-sur-Epte
By the early 10th century, the Carolingian king, Charles the Simple, realized that the Vikings, who had invaded in 800, would not go away quietly, so he ceded Rouen and the east of the region, making their leader Rollo the first duke of Normandy.

3 1066: Norman Conquest
When Edward the Confessor died without an heir, his cousin William saw his chance to claim the English throne. He sailed for England on 27 September 1066, triumphed at Hastings on 14 October, and was crowned King of England on Christmas Day.

Viking longship

4 1204: Union of Normandy and France
Since the accession of Henry II, King of England and Duke of Normandy, the French had tried to wrest control of the duchy from England. They succeeded in 1204, when King John lost Normandy to Philippe Auguste.

5 1315: Normandy Charter
Signed by Louis X, this charter gave the region provincial autonomy, a sovereign court of justice in Rouen, and control over taxes. In return, local taxes were increased dramatically – amounting to a quarter of the entire country's tax bill.

6 1450: French Recovery of Normandy
In the final phase of the Hundred Years' War, the decisive Battle of Formigny saw the French using guns and heavy cavalry to inflict a major defeat on English archers. This battle marked the end of fighting in Normandy and led to its recovery by France.

7 1789: Caen Revolt
During the French Revolution, there were royalist pockets throughout Normandy, but Caen became a centre for the republican Girondin movement (many of whose members originally came from the Gironde). Like the republicans who stormed the Bastille, their Norman counterparts demolished the château prison in Rouen.

For more on the Norman invasion of England **See pp12–15**

William the Conqueror with his army

Top 10 Historic Characters

1 Clovis
Merovingian King Clovis (465–511) founded the French state by defeating the Romans and uniting disparate tribes.

2 Rollo
After signing the Treaty of St-Clair-sur-Epte, Viking leader Hrølf (c.854–928) became Rollo, first duke of Normandy.

3 William Long Sword
Rollo's acquisitive warrior son (c.893–943) extended the duchy's boundaries by taking Cotentin and southern Manche.

4 William the Conqueror
William (1027–87), the bastard son of Robert the Magnificent, united Normandy and conquered England.

5 Matilda
Whilst abroad, William left Normandy in the hands of his wife Matilda (c.1031–83).

6 Richard the Lionheart
Richard (1157–99) became duke of Normandy in 1189. In 1196, he built Château Gaillard to protect Rouen.

7 Joan of Arc
A country girl (1412–31), she was encouraged by angelic voices to save France from English domination (see p23).

8 Samuel de Champlain
Explorer de Champlain (1567–1635) set out from Honfleur to found Quebec.

9 Charlotte Corday
Educated in Caen, Girondin sympathizer Corday (1768–93) killed radical revolutionary Jean-Paul Marat in his bath.

10 Charles de Gaulle
Leader of the Free French, de Gaulle (1890–1970) came ashore at Juno Beach on 14 June 1944 to reclaim France for the French.

8 1940: German Occupation
On 7 June 1940, the German army marched into Forges-les-Eaux and, two days later, into Rouen – the prelude to four years of occupation, during which local people were imprisoned, tortured, deported and executed.

9 1944: D-Day
In June 1944, Norman beaches became the target for Operation Overlord (see p31). By 20 August, the Allied forces were advancing towards Paris over the Perche hills.

10 2004: 60th Anniversary of D-Day
Every 10 years, surviving D-Day veterans gather to commemorate the dead; the 2004 gathering may have been one of the last.

Allied invasion of Normandy, 6 June 1944

For more on the D-Day landings See pp28–31

Left **Park Naturel Régional des Boucles de la Seine Normande** Right **La Suisse Normande**

🔟 Areas of Natural Beauty

Pays d'Auge

1 Pays d'Auge

When most people think of Normandy, they picture apple orchards, manor houses, rolling hills, hedgerows, meadows where brown and white cows graze, timbered farmhouses. This "typical Normandy" is the Pays d'Auge, the rural hinterland to the glamorous Côte Fleurie, and home to cider, Calvados and some of France's most famous cheeses, including Camembert. It is also home to Ste Thérèse of Lisieux, a long tradition of horse breeding, and a type of rice pudding called *teurgoule (see pp32–3).*

2 Parc Naturel Régional de Normandie-Maine

Normandy's largest regional park spans 2,350 sq km (900 sq miles) of Basse-Normandie and Pays de la Loire, with scenery that ranges from deep forests to gently rolling hills, and from marshlands to meadows. The park aims to preserve rural traditions by promoting local arts and crafts, agriculture, forestry and outdoor activities *(see p108).*

3 La Suisse Normande

Centred around the River Orne, this region of gentle hills, rocky cliffs, woods and charming villages is hardly reminiscent of Switzerland, but still attracts its share of hikers and tourists. Well placed for exploring, the capital Clécy is also a centre for climbing, canoeing and hang-gliding *(see p88).*

4 Parc Naturel Régional des Boucles de la Seine Normande

Following the snaking loops *(boucles)* of the Seine, this 580 sq km (224 sq mile) park wedged between Rouen and Le Havre was originally known as the Parc Naturel Régional de Brotonne. It embraces forests (notably the Forest of Brotonne), orchards, pastures and the Marais Vernier wetlands. It is also the starting point for the Fruit and Cottage Routes. ◈ *Map H3 • Maison du Parc: Notre-Dame-de-Bliquetuit. 02 35 37 23 16*

Pays de Caux

5 Pays de Caux

South of the striking white cliffs of the Côte d'Albâtre, and bordered by the fertile Seine and Bresle Valleys, this immense chalky plateau provides wonderfully rich soil for arable farmland. You can catch glimpses of the half-timbered buildings and apple orchards of the farmsteads through their massive stone gateways. ◈ *Map H1, H2*

6 Pays d'Ouche

As you journey from north to south, the landscape changes from the heavily wooded Eure to the lush, green countryside of the Orne. Spanning both, the Pays d'Ouche is blessed with abundant water. Streams, rivers and lakes make it something of a paradise for anglers. ◈ *Map G5, H5*

7 Parc Naturel Régional des Marais du Cotentin et du Bessin

The wetlands that characterize this park stretch 1,250 sq km (480 sq miles) from Les Veys to Lessay. The eastern marshes are home to many species of migrating birds and small mammals, which can be watched and studied from hides and nature reserves. ◈ *Map B3 • Maison du Parc: Les Ponts d'Ouve, St Côme du Mont. 02 33 71 65 30*

8 Pays de Bray

Occupying land in the northeast formed by a geological fault known as the *boutonnière* (buttonhole), Normandy's least populated area contains the Béthune, Andelle and Epte Rivers, and rich pasture perfect for dairy farming. ◈ *Map K2*

9 Parc Naturel Régional du Perche

Between the Beauce plains and the Pays de Bocage, this 1,820 sq km (700 sq mile) regional park was created in 1998. The high ground is forested; the lower slopes are planted with orchards and hedges. Châteaux and manor houses pepper the landscape. ◈ *Map H6 • For information: Manoir de Courboyer, Noce. 02 33 25 70 10*

Pays de Bocage

10 Pays de Bocage

From the south of Cotentin down to southwest Calvados, this is an intensely rural and unspoiled stretch of countryside, much loved by ramblers – a patchwork of meadows, interrupted only by woods, rivers, picturesque villages and the distinctive network of hedgerows that gives the region its name. ◈ *Map C4*

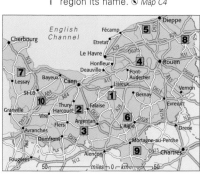

For more on forests **See pp66–7**

43

Left **Château de Bosmelet** Right **Château de Vandrimare**

TOP 10 Parks and Gardens

Jardins d' Argences

1 Jardins d'Argences
In a little valley near Coutances, the 17th-century Manoir d'Argences is surrounded by eight charming and distinctive gardens, connected by water. ✪ Saussey • Map B4 • Open late May–mid-Oct: 2–7pm daily • Adm charge

2 Jardin d'Elle
This is a modern landscaped garden with a maze of individually themed areas leading one into another, and more than 2,500 varieties of plants and trees on display. ✪ Villiers-Fossard • Map C4 • Open Feb–Nov: 10am–noon, 2–6pm Mon–Sat, 2–6pm Sun • Adm charge

3 Château de Brécy
Five terraces of formal gardens sweep gracefully from the château toward the focal point: an ornate wrought-iron gate bearing the initials of Brécy's 17th-century owners. The gardens are thought to have been designed by François Mansart. ✪ St-Gabriel-Brécy • Map D3 • Open Apr–Nov: 2:30–6:30pm Tue, Thu & Sun (Sat in Jun) • Adm charge

4 Château de Canon
The highlights of this 18th-century Anglo-French park, with its pretty, Italianate château, are the Chartreuses, a series of walled gardens brimming over with flowers. Statues, a temple and a Chinese pavilion add further interest. ✪ Mézidon-Canon • Map E4 • Open Easter–May: 2–6pm Sat & Sun; Jun–Sep: 2–6pm Wed–Mon • Adm charge

5 Jardin des Plantes, Rouen
These tranquil public gardens in the heart of the city house a large and important botanical collection, with formal flowerbeds, rare trees, hothouses, orangery, rose garden, rockery and a collection of medicinal plants. ✪ 114 av Martyrs de la Résistance • Map J3 • Open 8:30am–dusk daily • Free

Jardins des Plantes, Rouen

Château de Vandrimare

Each of these contemporary gardens is devoted to one of the five senses – sight, smell, sound, touch and taste. Set in a First Empire park, they include a maze, an orangery and over 2,500 plant species. ⊗ *Vandrimare • Map J3 • Open mid-Apr–mid-Nov: 2:30–6pm Mon & Fri, 10am–1pm, 2:30–6pm Sat & Sun • Adm charge*

Parc Zoologique Jean-Delacour

This landscaped park surrounds the Renaissance château at Clères. Created in 1920 by naturalist Jean Delacour, the garden is populated by flamingoes and exotic ducks, while in the park, animals such as kangaroos and gibbons roam in partial freedom. ⊗ *Clères • Map J2 • 02 35 33 23 08 • Open Feb–Oct: 10am–7pm daily; Nov: 1:30–5pm daily • Adm charge*

Château de Bosmelet

Built in Louis XIII style in 1632 (and restored after bombing in 1944), the château is notable for its "Rainbow Potager" (vegetable garden), a remarkable sight in summer. There is also a superb avenue of 300-year-old lime (linden) trees. ⊗ *Auffay • Map J2 • Open Jun, Sep: 1–7pm Fri, Sat & Sun; Jul–Aug: 1–7pm daily • Adm charge*

Jardins de Bellevue

Two national collections – of *Meconopsis* (Himalayan blue poppy) and *Helleborus Orientalis* (Lenten rose) – are included in these lovely year-round gardens facing the Forêt d'Eawy *(see p66)*. ⊗ *Beaumont-le-Hareng • Map J2 • 02 35 33 31 37 • Open 10am–6pm daily • Adm charge*

Jardins de Bellevue

Parc du Bois des Moutiers

Edwin Lutyens and Gertrude Jekyll created the park and gardens for Guillaume Mallet, for whom Lutyens also built the house in 1898. Between here and the sea, the *valleuse* (dry valley) is filled with acid-soil-loving plants such as rhododendrons and azaleas. Artists including Cocteau, Calder, Monet and Braque were frequent visitors in their day. ⊗ *Varengeville-sur-Mer • Map J1 • Open mid-Mar–mid-Nov: 10am–6pm daily • Adm charge*

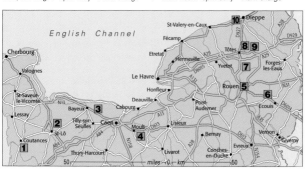

Left **Mont-St-Michel** Right **Abbaye-aux-Hommes, Caen**

Norman Abbeys

1 Mont-St-Michel
Dramatically sited on a lone rock in the Bay of Mont-St-Michel, this famous abbey exerts a huge draw on the thousands who visit every year *(see pp8–11)*.

2 Jumièges
A centre of learning for 700 years, Jumièges became nothing more than a quarry after the Revolution. Today, its enigmatic ruins, romantically set in a loop of the Seine, live again as one of the "must-see" sights of Normandy *(see pp18–19)*.

3 Le Bec-Hellouin
In 1034, a knight called Herluin exchanged his charger for a donkey and founded a religious community on the banks of the River Risle. When he was joined some eight years later by the influential Italian theologians Lanfranc and Anselm, the monastery grew to become the intellectual heart of Normandy. Disbanded in the Revolution and later demolished, it again became a Benedictine monastery in 1948 *(see pp89, 92)*.

4 Abbaye-aux-Hommes, Caen
Lanfranc was the first abbot of the abbey, which was founded by William the Conqueror and consecrated in his presence in 1077. Ten years later, William was buried, most unceremoniously, in the abbey's church, St-Etienne *(see p24)*.

Abbaye de Jumièges

5 Abbaye-aux-Dames, Caen
Like their founders William and Matilda, the Abbaye-aux-Hommes and Abbaye-aux-Dames (the first of the two to be built) are close cousins *(see p24)*. The lovely convent buildings were designed by Guillaume de la Tremblaye.

6 St-Georges, St-Martin-de-Boscherville
In 1114, William of Tancarville founded a small community of monks, who took this beautiful Norman Romanesque building as their abbey church *(see p80)*.

7 St-Wandrille
Founded in 649 and rebuilt in the 10th century after destruction by Norsemen, the abbey became a centre of learning. Inevitably, the Revolution saw its demise, but in 1931 it once again became a Benedictine monastery *(see p80)*.

For more on William the Conqueror **See p15**

8 La Trinité, Fécamp

This vast and austerely beautiful church owes its scale to a casket containing the Holy Blood of Christ, said to have been washed ashore in the trunk of a fig tree in the 1st century. The abbey built on the spot in the early 13th century attracted streams of pilgrims. Le Précieux Sang is still venerated today *(see p78)*.

9 Hambye

Lord of the Manor Guillaume Paynel founded the abbey in 1145. Always a small community, its fortunes declined over the years, and in 1784 it was declared defunct. In the 19th century, the buildings were quarried for stone; only in the 20th were the noble ruins we see today saved from further destruction *(see p98)*.

10 La Trappe

Founded in 1140, La Trappe was one of the Cistercian monasteries which adopted the Strict Observance – silence, prayer, abstinence, manual labour – introduced by Abbé de Rancé in the 1660s. Thereafter, they were known as Trappist monasteries; there is another at Briquebec *(see p100)*. ◈ Soligny-la-Trappe • Map F5, H5

Abbaye St-Georges, St-Martin-de-Boscherville

Top 10 Religious Figures

1 St Ouen

Credited with reviving Christian zeal in the Rouen region, as a result of which several abbeys were founded.

2 St Philibert

Gascon court favourite and protégé of St Ouen. Founded Jumièges in the 7th century.

3 St Wandrille

The nobleman founder (in 649) of the eponymous abbey. Known as God's True Athlete for his remarkable physique.

4 St Aubert

Bishop of Avranches, to whom, legend has it, the Archangel Gabriel appeared in 708, ordering him to build a chapel on Mont St-Michel.

5 Lanfranc

Influential Italian lawyer-monk (1005–1089). Became William the Conqueror's Archbishop at Canterbury.

6 St Anselm

Philosopher-monk (1033–1109) who joined Lanfranc at Bec and succeeded him as Archbishop of Canterbury.

7 Joan of Arc

Teenage soldier (1412–31) whose "voices" told her to save France from the English. Captured and burnt at the stake. Canonized in 1920.

8 Guillaume de la Tremblaye

Benedictine monk at Bec, who was a master architect and sculptor (1644–1715).

9 Abbot de Rancé

Nobleman who renounced his former life and founded the Trappists in 1664.

10 St Thérèse Martin

Deeply spiritual young nun (1873–97) whose shrine at Lisieux is venerated.

For more on Joan of Arc **See p23**

Raoul Dufy, *Le Quinze Août* (detail), 1931

🔟 Artists in Normandy

Claude Monet, *Chemin de la Cavée*

1 Claude Monet
The founder and leading light of Impressionism was brought up in Le Havre. Having moved to Paris, he returned regularly to paint in Honfleur, Rouen, Étretat and Varengeville. In 1883 he settled in Giverny, where he spent the rest of his life *(see pp34–7)*.

2 JMW Turner
The greatest English land-scape artist of his time, Turner (1775–1851) paid frequent visits to Dieppe, Le Havre, Rouen and the Seine estuary. His vibrant watercolours had a profound influence on the young Monet.

3 Théodore Géricault
Born into a rich Rouen family, Géricault (1791–1824) shocked contemporaries with the realism of paintings such as *The Raft of the Medusa*.

4 Pierre-Auguste Renoir
Monet's great friend and fellow Impressionist, Renoir (1841–1919), did not discover Normandy until he came to the coast in 1879, the year he painted *Cliffs at Pourville* and *Mussel Collectors at Berneval*. Once Monet had settled in Giverny, Renoir was a regular visitor.

5 Jean-François Millet
Son of a peasant farmer in Gréville-Hague, Millet (1814–75) was apprenticed to a painter in Cherbourg before moving to Paris, where he worked under Paul Delaroche, and later to Barbizon, where he became a member of the Barbizon School led by Théodore Rousseau. He is best known for his naturalistic paintings of farm workers.

6 Jean-Baptiste Corot
Corot (1796–1875) was a landscape painter who turned to portrait painting late in his career. The picturesque town of Étretat *(see p78)* had particular appeal for him, and he travelled there with Courbet in the 1860s and '70s.

7 Gustave Courbet
First and most significant of the French Realists, Gustave Courbet (1819–77) spent time in Trouville with the American artist Whistler, as well as accompanying Corot to Étretat. His series of stormy seascapes, with changing skies, was a great influence on the Impressionists.

For more on Monet **See pp34–7**

8 Raoul Dufy
Only after flirtations with Impressionism and Fauvism did Dufy (1877–1953), a native of Le Havre, find his own style, using vivid, pure colour. His favourite subjects include carefree, ephemeral scenes on beaches, at horse races or regattas, and in the coastal towns of Normandy.

9 Eugène Boudin
Brought up under the vast, luminous sky of Honfleur, Boudin (1824–98) did not have to travel far to paint his land- and sea-scapes. An advocate of painting in the open air – a practice to which he introduced Monet – he was preoccupied with light and its effects on his subject matter. His loose brush-strokes heralded Impressionist techniques.

10 Georges Braque
Braque (1882–1963), who learned to paint while working for his decorator father in Le Havre, was initially attracted to the Fauve artists, but an encounter with Picasso transformed his style. In later years, he painted local landscapes and made stained glass in a studio in Varengeville.

Georges Braque, *The House*

Top 10 Paintings of Normandy

1 Rouen Cathedral Series (Monet)
Painted between 1891 and 1895. One is displayed in the Musée des Beaux-Arts, Rouen, others in the Musée d'Orsay, Paris.

2 Water Lily Series (Monet)
Painted between 1899 and 1926. Several are on show at the Musée d'Orangerie, Paris.

3 Impression: Sunrise (Monet)
Painted in Le Havre in 1872. Displayed in the Musée Marmottan, Paris.

4 The Gleaners (Millet)
Painted in 1857. Exhibited at the Musée d'Orsay, Paris.

5 The Cliff at Étretat after the Storm (Courbet)
Painted in 1869. Displayed in the Musée d'Orsay, Paris.

6 Wheat-field in Normandy (Dufy)
Painted in 1935. On show at the Musée Eugène Boudin, Honfleur.

7 People on the Beach at Trouville (Boudin)
Painted in 1865. Exhibited at the Musée Eugène Boudin, Honfleur.

8 View from the Port of Dieppe (Pissarro)
Painted in 1902. Displayed in the Château-Musée de Dieppe.

9 The Fish Market, Honfleur (Dubourg)
Painted in 1876. Displayed in the Musée Eugène Boudin, Honfleur.

10 View of the Coast of Normandy (Richard Bonnington)
Painted in 1823. Exhibited at the Louvre, Paris.

For more on Honfleur artists See p17

Left **Jules Barbey d'Aurevilly** Right **Marcel Proust**

Writers in Normandy

Gustave Flaubert
Flaubert spent the greater part of his 59 years in Normandy; its places and people suffuse his writing. Born in Rouen in 1821, he abandoned a Paris law training to live and write in Croisset until his death. He published his finest work, *Madame Bovary*, in 1857.

Guy de Maupassant
Maupassant (1850–93) was born at Château de Miromesnil near Dieppe, and spent his childhood in Étretat. His mother had been a playmate of Flaubert, who guided Maupassant's debut as a writer. His first masterpiece was *Boule de suif* (1880).

Marcel Proust
Proust was born in Paris in 1871 and died there in 1922. His *A la recherche du temps perdu* is permeated by memories of Normandy – perhaps most notably the Grand Hôtel at Cabourg *(see p27)*, which he renamed Balbec.

Pierre Corneille

Pierre Corneille
The classical dramatist Pierre Corneille (1606–84) was born in Rouen. His plays *Le Cid*, *Horace*, *Cinna* and *Polyeucte* formed the yardstick for French tragedy, while *Le Menteur* is a comic masterpiece. His writing often reflects the tension between regional and national loyalties.

André Gide
Born in 1869 of a Huguenot father and Norman mother, Gide spent the early and latter parts of his life in Normandy. He saw the realities of life here, first as mayor of a commune, and later as a juror in Rouen. He won the Nobel prize four years before his death in 1951.

Jules Barbey d'Aurevilly
Barbey (1808–89), novelist, commentator, conversationalist and, as an admirer of Byron and Brummell, inveterate dandy, was still able to scandalize at 66, when he published *Les Diaboliques*. Born in St-Saveur-le-Vicomte, he was raised on a diet of Norman tales told by a family servant.

Alain Chartier
Pasquier called Alain Chartier (c.1390–c.1430) – probably best known for *La Belle Dame sans merci* – "the Seneca of France". Born into a distinguished Bayeux family, he wrote his earliest poem, *Livre des quatre dames*, after France's defeat at the Battle of Agincourt in 1415.

8 Robert Wace

What little is known about the poet Robert Wace (c.1115–c.1183) comes from his last work, *Roman de Rou*, a verse history of the dukes of Normandy. Educated in Caen, he wrote his romances for the great and good there.

9 François Malherbe

The classical poet Malherbe (1555–1628) left his birthplace Caen to study in Paris, Basle and Heidelberg. He worked for Henri d'Angoulême (*grand prieur* of France and governor of Provence) for 10 years before returning home. Called to Court in 1605, he became the strict arbiter of French literary style.

François Malherbe

10 Jacques Prévert

Prévert (1900–77) visited Normandy in 1930 and fell in love with it. Soon after, he started to write poetry on the themes of beauty, innocence, love and despair. *Paroles*, his best-known collection, was published in 1945. In 1971, he and his wife bought a house in Omonville-la-Petite. They are buried nearby, and there is a memorial garden in St-Germain-des-Vaux *(see p101)*.

Top 10 Books Set in Normandy

1 Madame Bovary (Gustave Flaubert)
Set near the author's native Rouen, this classic ruffled contemporary feathers.

2 A Day in the Country and Other Stories (Guy de Maupassant)
Twenty-eight of Maupassant's brilliant short stories.

3 The Secret Life of the Seine (Mort Rosenblum)
From Burgundy to Le Havre by houseboat.

4 A Woman's Story (Annie Ernaux)
A lovely tribute to the author's mother, who lived much of her life in Yvetot.

5 The Bayeux Tapestry (Wolfgang Grape)
The Norman Conquest as told through the Bayeux Tapestry.

6 Mont-St-Michel and Chartres (Henry Brooks Adams)
Meditation on the medieval world as seen through its most famous cathedrals.

7 Operation Overlord (Max Hastings)
Goes beyond D-Day to cover the ensuing battles, viewing the conflict from both sides.

8 Gardens in Normandy (Valery, Motte and Sarramon)
Forty spectacular gardens.

9 Chantemesle: A Normandy Childhood (Robin Fedden)
A lyrical account of an enchanted rural childhood.

10 A Normandy Tapestry (Alan Biggins)
Biggins' move to France with his family took him behind the scenes of French rural life.

Bayeux Tapestry

Museums and Galleries

Bayeux Tapestry
Embroidered in 1077, this much-loved treasure unfolds, with astonishing detail, clarity and drama, the story of Duke William's conquest of England. The galleries leading up to the tapestry bring the historical background vividly to life. The cloth itself – all 70 m (230 ft) of it – is displayed behind glass *(see pp12–13)*.

Le Mémorial de Caen
A moving and contemplative museum of remembrance, the Mémorial takes the visitor on a journey through the causes and consequences of World War II and the ensuing Cold War, using a host of interactive and audio-visual techniques, as well as fascinating archive footage. An extension to the museum acts as a place of reflection on peace and the means of achieving it *(see pp24–5)*.

Cité de la Mer, Cherbourg
This attraction is extremely popular, so in high season it's wise to arrive as early in the day as possible. The former maritime

Cité de la Mer, Cherbourg

station is now home to Europe's deepest aquarium. An added attraction is *Le Redoutable*, the first visitable French nuclear-powered submarine (built at Cherbourg). All of this introduces the visitor to the wonders of the underwater world, and to human adventures and achievements there. Allow three hours for your visit. ⚓ *Gare Maritime Transatlantique, Cherbourg • Map B2 • Open Feb–Jun: 9:30am–6pm daily; Jul–Aug: 9:30am–7pm daily; Sep–Dec: 10am–6pm daily. Closed Christmas, New Year, 2 weeks Jan • Adm charge*

Musée des Impression-nismes, Giverny
This museum is the only one in France that is wholly devoted to the important and influential Impressionist movement. It aims to explore the international nature of Impressionism *(see pp34, 36)*.

Musée des Beaux-Arts, Rouen
Monet's study of Rouen Cathedral and Corot's fine *Quayside Trade in Rouen* are among the highlights of this important art museum, strong on Old Masters as well as the Impressionists *(see p22)*.

Musée Eugène Boudin, Honfleur
Honfleur's rich artistic heritage is celebrated in this appealing museum, which includes works by Boudin himself, as well as by Monet *(see p16)*.

7 Musée du Mobilier Miniature, Vendeuvre

Unique in its extent and quality, this extraordinary collection of miniature furniture is housed in the orangery of Château de Vendeuvre. The exquisite pieces – which include *objets* such as cutlery, porcelain, paintings and chess sets – date from the 16th to 19th centuries, and are fascinating for their meticulous detail and craftsmanship *(see p33)*.

Musée du Mobilier Miniature, Vendeuvre

8 Musée des Beaux-Arts, Caen

Standing within the walls of William the Conqueror's hilltop château, Caen's fine art collection is housed in a well-lit contemporary building. French, Italian, Flemish and Dutch paintings, chronologically arranged from the 15th to the 20th centuries, present a coherent survey of the history of painting. Perugino's *The Marriage of the Virgin* is a highlight *(see p24)*.

Musée Malraux, Le Havre

9 Musée Malraux, Le Havre

This innovative building of glass and metal, offering views of the port through a monumental concrete sculpture known as "The Eye", is filled with light. Inside, the galleries are linked by gangways. There are fine collections by Raoul Dufy and Eugène Boudin. ◎ *2 blvd Clemenceau, Le Havre • Map E2 • Open 11am–6pm Wed–Fri & Mon, 11am–7pm Sat & Sun • Adm charge*

10 Musee de Beaux-Arts et de la Dentelle, Alençon

In 1665, lacemakers in Alençon were given the challenge of creating lace equal in quality and popular appeal to that of Venice. They succeeded, coming up with a new and better technique, which made Alençon lace supreme until demand dropped in the 20th century. The story is told here, along with exquisite and intricate examples of the craft. ◎ *Cour Carrée de la Dentelle, Alençon • Map E6 • Open 10am–noon, 2–6pm Tue–Sun (Jul–Aug: open daily) • Adm charge*

Left **Teurgoule** Right **Tripes à la mode de Caen**

🔟 Culinary Highlights

1 Poulet Vallée d'Auge
The key Norman ingredients, cider and cream, are combined to make this delicious chicken dish from the Pays d'Auge. Chicken pieces and mushrooms are sautéed in butter, then braised in a sauce of cider, Calvados and cream. Other classic Norman dishes served in a sauce of cider and cream are *côtes de veau* (veal cutlets) and *filet de porc* (pork fillet).

2 Omelette de la Mère Poulard
Annette Poulard (1861–1931) was the *patronne* of a hotel on Mont-St-Michel. The exact recipe for her famously perfect omelettes, available at any time of the day to hungry visitors who had crossed the bay on foot or by horse and cart, is not known. We do know, however, that she never let the butter brown, beat the eggs vigorously in a copper bowl, possibly separating the yolks and whites first, and stirred continuously as she cooked them in her long-handled pan.

3 Teurgoule
An enormously popular dessert, both at home and in restaurants, this regional speciality dates back to the days when spices, brought back to Honfleur and Dieppe by merchant ships from the East, first became popular.

Local housewives discovered that a flavouring of cinnamon was the perfect partner for pudding rice baked with cream, and *teurgoule* was born.

4 Marmite Dieppoise
This hearty fish stew was originally concocted in Dieppe as a way of using up the many different types of fish, as well as shrimps and mussels, that were readily available. Like *teurgoule*, it is lightly flavoured with spices.

5 Filets de sole Normande
Occupying pride of place amongst the catch brought back by Normandy's fishermen is the magnificent Dover sole, in French, *sole Normande*. It is equally delicious cooked simply, with butter (*à la meunière*), or, as in Dieppe, with shrimps and mussels in a creamy *velouté* sauce – or prepared in countless other ways.

Filets de sole

For tips on eating and drinking **See p120**

6 Canard à la Rouennaise

Tasting much better than it sounds, *canard à la Rouennaise* refers to ducklings that have been dispatched by smothering; as a result, the blood is prevented from escaping, giving a strong flavour to the meat. Traditionally, the bird is stuffed, then served in a sauce made of its own liver and blood.

7 Tripes à la mode de Caen

A popular country dish in Normandy, tripe from the excellent local cattle is cooked simply *à la mode de Caen* with onions, calf's feet, Calvados and cider, while in Ferté-Macé it is made into little bundles *en brochette* (on skewers).

8 Caille aux monstrueux

There are many ways to cook this speciality of Elbeuf, but the two essential ingredients are quail and leeks. The variety of leek cultivated in the Seine and Eure Valleys is known as *monstrueux* (literally, "monstrous" – they are short and fat), and their distinctive flavour perfectly complements the quail.

9 Douillons and Bourdelots

Most often found in cake shops rather than in restaurants, these individual, melt-in-the-mouth pastries are each filled with a whole small apple or pear, peeled and cored and flavoured with cinnamon.

10 Trou Normand

This famous Norman speciality – or rather indulgence – refers to a shot of chilled Calvados thrown back between courses to aid digestion. The word *trou* means "hole": the shot of *calva*, Normans fondly believe, creates a hole for more food.

Top 10 Cheeses

1 Camembert
This world-famous cheese was invented by Marie Harel during the Revolution. By the 1880s, equipped with its famous box and label, it was being exported all over Europe.

2 Livarot
Another cheese with a long history, it tastes a great deal better than it smells.

3 Neufchâtel
Dating back to the 10th century, this creamy cheese comes as a heart, or in one of five other shapes.

4 Pont l'Evêque
Originally called Angelot, this square, washed rind cheese, matured in wooden boxes, dates back to the Middle Ages.

5 Pavé d'Auge
Square, spicy cheese from the northern Pays d'Auge – a forerunner of Pont l'Evêque.

6 Brillat-Savarin
A triple-cream cheese invented by cheese-maker Henri Androuët.

7 Fin-de-siècle
Despite its name, the history of this triple-cream cheese, promoted by Androuët, is unknown.

8 Fromage de Monsieur
A strong cheese invented near Rouen and sold by a man whose name really was M Fromage (Mr Cheese).

9 Coutances
Packaged in a round box, this rich, creamy cheese has a thin crust.

10 Briquebec
This mild cheese was invented in the 19th century by the Trappist monks of the Abbaye de Briquebec in the *département* of Manche.

 For restaurant listings **See pp56–57, 83, 95, 103, 113**

Left **Château de Sully, Bayeux** Right **Hôtel de la Marine, Barneville-Carteret**

🔟 Gourmet Restaurants

1 La Chaîne d'Or, Les Andelys

This enveloping 18th-century inn offers excellent traditional cooking and fine river views. The *menu détente* is very reasonably priced. ⍟ *25–27 rue Grande • Map J3 • 02 32 54 00 31 • Closed Wed L • €€€*

Manoir du Lys, Bagnoles-de-l'Orne

2 Manoir du Lys, Bagnoles-de-l'Orne

Franck Quinton's cooking is rooted in local tradition but respects contemporary trends. He loves truffles and mushrooms, and organizes popular "mushroom weekends". Dine outside or take a *digestif* in the cosy salon. ⍟ *La Croix Gauthier, rte de Juvigny-sous-Andaine • Map D5 • 02 33 37 80 69 • Closed Mon L, Tue L, Jan–mid-Feb; Sun D (Nov–Apr); Mon D, Wed L (May–Oct) • €€€*

3 Hôtel de la Marine, Barneville-Carteret

From his *beignet de foie gras en vinaigrette de betterave* to his *brioche aux pommes confites*, Laurent Cesne's distinctive blend of innovation and delicacy has won him many admirers. Several of his specialities feature fish or shellfish. ⍟ *11 rue de Paris • Map A3 • 02 33 53 83 31 • Closed Mon L (Jan, Apr–Sep, Nov–Dec), Sun D, Mon (Feb, Mar, Oct) • €€€*

4 Château de Sully, Bayeux

This handsome château hotel has the finest restaurant in the area. In the grand dining room, with its chandeliers and panelled walls, the freshest local produce is served in elegant and tempting ways (see p127). ⍟ *rte de Port-en-Bessin • Map D3 • 02 31 22 29 48 • Closed lunch except Sun, Dec–mid-Jan • €€€€*

5 Pavé d'Auge, Beuvron-en-Auge

The former covered market of this picturesque village is the setting for the Pays d'Auge's most sophisticated restaurant, where luxurious dishes (featuring langoustines, asparagus and foie gras) and fine wines are served. ⍟ *pl du Village • Map E3 • 02 31 79 26 71 • Closed Mon–Tue, Dec • €€€*

6 Manoir de la Drôme, Balleroy

The garden at this old mill is the ideal spot for an elegant meal. Denis Leclerc's menus are sumptuous, but be ready to leave them aside to try one of the specials created from the best ingredients of the day, like John Dory with wild mushrooms. ⍟ *129 rue des Forges • Map C3 • 02 31 21 60 94 • Closed Tue L, Sun D, Mon, Wed, mid-Feb–mid-Mar • €€€€€*

Unless otherwise stated, all restaurants accept credit cards and serve vegetarian meals.

7 La Terrasse et l'Assiette, Honfleur

A relaxed and convivial place, run by chef Gérard Bonnefoy and his wife Anne-Marie. M Bonnefoy is a master of classic cooking with a contemporary twist: seductive and beautifully presented. ◈ *8 pl Ste-Catherine • Map F3 • 02 31 89 31 33 • Closed Mon, Jan • €€€*

8 Sa.Qua.Na, Honfleur

The name is short for "Saveurs (Flavours), Qualité, Nature". Chef Alexandre Bourdas has an adventurous approach, combining Japanese and other influences with the finest local produce. Decor is modern and very chic. ◈ *22 pl Hamelin • Map F3 • 02 31 89 40 80 • Closed lunch (except Sat & Sun), Wed, Thu • €€€€€*

9 Gill, Rouen

With two Michelin stars, Gill is Normandy's foremost gourmet establishment. In the elegant quayside dining room, the best of Norman produce is transformed into concoctions such as *pigeon à la rouennaise avec ses raviolis de foie gras*. ◈ *8–9 quai de la Bourse • Map L6 • 02 35 71 16 14 • Closed first 2 weeks of Jan • €€€€*

10 Les Nymphéas, Rouen

Locals are drawn mainly by the imaginative cuisine – in particular, the wide selection of fish. ◈ *7–9 rue de la Pie • Map L5 • 02 35 89 26 69 • Closed Tue L, Sun D, Mon • €€€*

The elegant interior of Gill, Rouen

Top 10 Norman Produce

1 Apples and Pears
Normandy's fertile soil supports countless varieties, used widely in cooking, and for cider, Calvados and sparkling *poiré*.

2 Vegetables
Manche is renowned for its superb carrots, parsley, leeks, radishes and shallots.

3 Dairy Products
The rich milk produced by Norman cattle makes velvety cream, butter (*beurre d'Isigny* is highly prized), and products ranging from Petit-Suisse cream cheese to *confiture de lait*, literally, "milk jam".

4 Cheese
Four great soft cheeses – Camembert, Pont l'Evêque, Neufchâtel and Livarot – star on the Norman cheese board.

5 Agneau de pré-salé
Lamb raised on the salt marshes around Mont-St-Michel has a deliciously delicate flavour.

6 Boudin noir
Black pudding is the speciality of Mortagne-au-Perche (see p72).

7 Andouille
Equally highly prized is the black tripe sausage produced in Vire.

8 Fish
The Atlantic waters yield superb fish, supreme among which is the Dover sole.

9 Oysters
Norman oysters come from beds in one of three *crus*, or areas: Côte Ouest, St-Vaast-la-Hougue and Isigny.

10 Pork
Pale-fleshed Norman pork is highly prized, particularly *porc de Bayeux*.

Left **Dieppe Market** Right **Caen Market**

🔟 Markets

1 L'Aigle
Noisy and bustling, this huge market draws thousands of people to L'Aigle every Tuesday. Hundreds of stalls, piled high with regional bounty from fruit and vegetables to cheeses and cider, are crammed into the town centre. Meanwhile, the livestock market (7:30–9:30am), the third largest in France, provides raucous accompaniment; it's not for the tender-hearted. ◈ Map H5

Caen Market

2 Caen
Handsome 18th-century houses line place St-Sauveur, the square in the centre of Caen where the pillory once stood, and where the colourful Friday market has been held since 1026. Stall-holders sell traditional produce and, for early risers, an amazing selection of fresh fish. ◈ Map L2

3 Dieppe
Each Saturday, from 8am until noon, the long, pedestrian Grande Rue, lined with some 200 shops, becomes a massive open-air emporium. Locals set up stalls to sell their produce (organic fruit and vegetables, *saucisses*, jams),

professionals bring imports (olives, honey, exotic cheeses) from every corner of France, and fishermen sell their daily catches. Dieppe is famous for its *lisettes* (baby mackerel), scallops and *gendarmes*, the smoked herrings available in November. ◈ Map J1

4 Rouen
Place St-Marc is the scene of a lively market on Tuesday, Friday, Saturday and Sunday, with fruit, veg, bric-à-brac and second-hand book stalls. From 24 November, there's a Christmas market in place de la Cathédrale. Stalls resembling chalets sell gastronomic specialities and arts and crafts. Among the events are concerts and pony rides. ◈ Map N6

5 Dives-sur-Mer
Shopping in the traditional Saturday market in Dives is an event, not least because it is held in the spectacular timbered *halles* with a red-tiled roof, built in the 15th century so that the local monastery could levy market taxes. In July and August there is also a small market on Tuesdays featuring regional products. ◈ Map E3

St-Pierre-sur-Dives Market

St-Pierre-sur-Dives

Like Dives-sur-Mer, this inland town has a magnificent covered market hall. Dating from the 11th century, it was the largest medieval hall in Normandy. After it burned down in 1944, it was completely rebuilt in the style of the original, using hundreds of thousands of wooden pegs instead of screws and nails. Small local producers bring their goods to the Monday market, which spills out of the hall. ⊗ Map E4

Cambremer Market

Bayeux

One edge of the market that fills place St-Patrice every Saturday morning is devoted to local smallholders, their home-grown fruit and vegetables, home-produced cheese and sausages, and their livestock: perhaps a few geese, chickens and a litter of puppies. The other stallholders are professional retailers, selling clothes as well as food. ⊗ Map D3

St-Lô

There's a typical farmers' market on Saturday mornings in the main square of this ancient and historic town. Here you can buy fresh produce from local farmers and fishermen among the stalls selling furniture, clothing and flowers. ⊗ Map C4

Forges-les-Eaux

An excellent farmers' market is held on Thursday mornings in the town centre and Sunday mornings in Halle Baltard in this spa town on the Route du Fromage de Neufchâtel (see p60). Stalls offer organic dairy products, eggs, smoked meat and fish, jam and the Pays de Bray cheeses including the famous Neufchâtel. On Thursday, there is a livestock market as well. ⊗ Map K2

Cambremer

Local people dressed in peasant costumes, folk dancing, music-making and horse-drawn carriage rides are all part of the fun at Cambremer's traditional market, staged every Sunday morning in the market place in July and August and on special occasions such as Easter, 1 May and Whit Sunday. Local producers mingle with regional craftsmen and artists. ⊗ Map E4

Left **Falaise d'Aval, Étretat** Right **Deauville**

Spas and Resorts

1 Forges-les-Eaux

Quiet and dignified, Forges-les-Eaux became a fashionable spa town after it was visited in 1633 by a regal threesome: Louis XIII, his queen, Anne of Austria, and Cardinal Richelieu. Today, the spa and casino, built in the 1950s, are run as a health and leisure complex by Groupe Partouche. ◈ *Map K2*

2 Étretat

With its shingle beach and esplanade curving between two famous chalk headlands, the Falaises d'Aval and d'Amont, its dramatic clifftop walks and its recreational Parc de Loisirs des Roches, charming and elegant Étretat is the Côte d'Albâtre's most alluring resort, as many writers and artists discovered in the 19th century *(see p78)*.

Riva-Bella

3 Deauville and La Côte Fleurie

The magnificent coastline from Honfleur to Cabourg, with its series of wide, sandy beaches, means that all of its resorts – Villerville, Trouville, Deauville, Villers-sur-Mer, Houlgate and Cabourg – have much to offer the sun-worshipper, with swimming and watersports all the way along. If you tire of the sun, and your money is burning a hole in your pocket, you will find no shortage of casinos to lose it in. Each place has its own character, none more so than exclusive Deauville *(see pp26–7)*.

4 Riva-Bella

The people of Caen, on the River Orne, are proud of their close connection to the sea, and here, at the mouth of the river, is "Caen-sur-Mer": the attractive ferry and yachting port of Ouistreham and the bustling resort of Riva-Bella, with its superb sandy beach and jolly main street, rue de la Mer. ◈ *Map E3*

5 Luc-sur-Mer

Thalassotherapy (sea-water treatment) is a speciality of Norman resorts, and at bracing Luc-sur-Mer, the cure uses kelp extract. There's also a sea-water hammam. Children can shore-fish for crabs, shrimps and clams, and admire the skeleton of a 19 m (76 ft) beached whale on display in the attractive municipal park. ◈ *Map D3*

Courseulles-sur-Mer

A little further west along the Côte de Nacre at Juno Beach, where memories of the Normandy Invasion *(see pp28–31)* mingle with modern-day seaside amusements, Courseulles has a large marina (somewhat over-shadowed by modern apartment blocks), and a terrific shellfish aquarium. Just inland is Reviers, where an arts and crafts festival takes place each July. ◈ *Map D3*

Barneville-Plage

Spectacular sandy beaches, backed by windblown dunes, sweep along the west coast of the Cotentin Peninsula, looking out toward the Channel Islands. At Barneville-Plage, between busy Barneville-Carteret and charming Portbail, the coastline becomes tame enough for a holiday beach, full to bursting in summer, and backed by lines of villas *(see p100)*.

Agon-Coutainville

With its 8 km (5 miles) of fine, sandy beach, this west coast resort makes a great summer playground for the people of nearby Coutances and visitors alike. Contrast a morning on the beach with a walk out to Pointe d'Agon, with its magnificent sea views. ◈ *Map B4*

Bagnoles de l'Orne

Granville

With its stern granite upper town on the one hand, and its beach and seaside amusements on the other, Granville offers two quite different faces. It became fashionable as a resort in the 19th century. Among its current attractions, it boasts a thalasso-therapy centre, the Aquarium du Roc (a "shell wonderland") and a casino *(see p98)*.

Bagnoles-de-l'Orne

Legend has it that Hugues de Tessé left his horse Rapide to die quietly of old age in the forest, only for the animal to trot home in rude health. He found that a spring was the cause, bathed there himself, and was also re-juvenated. Today, this calm, orderly spa town attracts thousands to its Établissement Thermal, particularly helpful for rheumatism and circulatory problems *(see p107)*.

Left **Maison Henry IV, St-Valéry-en-Caux** Right **St-Céneri-le-Gérei**

Unspoilt Villages

Barfleur

Barfleur
The long tradition of fishing in Normandy is perfectly embodied in the charming port of Barfleur. Stubby, brightly painted fishing boats jostle in the harbour, overlooked by stern granite houses braced for all weathers. Beaches for shell gathering and a lighthouse you can climb make it a perfect place to visit *(see p101)*.

St-Fraimbault
Saint-Fraimbault is a true *village fleurie*. Each spring, 100,000 flowers swamp the village in colour as villagers try to outdo each other's displays. It all culminates in a mid-August festival. ✪ *Map D6*

St-Céneri-le-Gérei
This ravishing village has a memorable setting. Crowned by a fine Romanesque church, its stone houses overlook the gentle River Sarthe as it flows around a rocky promontory on the edge of the Alpes Mancelles *(see p110)*.

Beuvron-en-Auge
All the charms of the Pays d'Auge are summed up in Beuvron. Its flower-decked houses are prettily striped and patterned with timber. On the south side of the central square, the delightful 15th-century Vieux Manoir is elaborately decorated with wood carvings *(see p33)*.

Putot-en-Auge
This sleepy Pays d'Auge village has little more than a church (with a fine Romanesque portal, and a cemetery for Allied soldiers), manor house and little brick-built *mairie* (town hall), but it somehow encapsulates the rural delights of the Auge region. Nearby Criqueville-en-Auge is also worth a visit for its enchanting manor house. ✪ *Map E3*

St-Fraimbault

Lyons-la-Forêt

A captivating medley of 16th- to 18th-century half-timbered buildings, Lyons-la-Forêt stands in a sylvan setting deep in the lovely Forêt de Lyons. It starred in both the 1934 Jean Renoir and the 1991 Claude Chabrol versions of *Madame Bovary*, whose intangible influence still permeates the area *(see pp50, 79)*.

Montville

At the confluence of two rivers – Clérette and Cailly – Montville is distinctive for flowers and fire engines. A *village fleurie*, it has an attractive lake, a park with a superb 300-year-old purple beech, and the Musée des Sapeurs-Pompiers (museum of the fire brigade), full of old hand pumps and gleaming red fire engines. It traces the history of the French fire brigade from the early 18th century onwards. ✪ *Map J2*

Allouville-Bellefosse

An extraordinary oak tree, thought to be at least 1,300 years old, has put this little village on the map. Inside the huge trunk are a sanctuary and a hermit's cell fashioned by a local priest in 1696. Nearby, in an old farmhouse deep in the countryside, is the Musée de la Nature, dedicated to the local landscape, flora and fauna. ✪ *Map H2*

Le Bec-Hellouin

A quintessential Norman village set among fields and apple orchards, Le Bec-Hellouin takes its name from the stream that runs

Allouville-Bellefosse

beside it and from the Norman knight Herluin, founder of the impressive 11th-century Benedictine abbey. Half-timbered houses and colourful window boxes add to the charm. ✪ *Map H2*

St-Valéry-en-Caux

Encircled by high cliffs, this fishing village as well as child-friendly seaside resort occupies a charming spot on the Côte d'Albâtre, where tranquil Pays de Caux countryside meets beach, boats and bikinis. It is graced by the Maison Henri IV, a fine, timber-framed Renaissance house on the quay. ✪ *Map H11*

Left **Pottery** Right **Lacemaking**

Arts and Crafts

1 Pottery

With good-quality clay and a constant demand for jugs and mugs in which to serve cider and milk, there is a long tradition of pottery-making in Normandy. At the Musée de la Poterie in Ger (between Flers and Mortain), you can see how the craft has developed over 500 years, and watch a potter at work. In Noron-la-Poterie near Bayeux, salt-glaze pottery has been made since the Middle Ages; several studios are still in operation. The painted earthenware of Forges-les-Eaux is on display in the Musée de Faïence there.

2 Rouen Faïence

Faïence (earthenware with a white tin glaze that can then be decorated) was introduced to Rouen by Masséot Abaquesne in the mid-16th century. It flowered into a fine art, before ceasing in the 1780s with the advent of imported chinaware. Beautiful examples can be seen in the Musée de la Céramique in Rouen *(see p22)*, and modern copies are on sale all over town *(see p82)*.

Rouen Faïence earthenware

3 Roof Finials

In Normandy, *épis de faitage*, often coloured and ending either in a simple point or topped by a bird, are much admired. Seen to best effect on the fantastical 19th-century villas of Deauville, they can also be spotted in the Bayeux Tapestry. You could have one too: at Poterie du Mesnil de Bavent in Ranville, ceramic finials have been hand-produced since 1842 *(see p94)*.

4 Lacemaking

From the 17th to 19th centuries, lace was all the rage across Europe. In Normandy, Alençon, Argentan and Bayeux were the three main centres of production, each with their own technique. Exquisite examples can be seen in all three towns, while Bayeux's bobbin lace with its intricate floral motif is still made by a dedicated group of craftswomen *(see p14)*.

5 Traditional Furniture

Highly regarded, Norman antique furniture is characterized by four objects: the wardrobe (traditionally part of a bride's dowry), the sideboard, the longcase clock and the box bed. Fine 18th- and 19th-century pieces, on display in museums and for sale in antiques shops, are well proportioned, elegant and often elaborately decorated.

6 Wooden Toys

In Bézu-Saint-Eloi, 6 km (4 miles) northwest of Gisors, Ateliers Jorelle have been making

Wooden toys, Ateliers Jorelle

traditional wooden toys since 1864. Visit the workshop, or look out for their products in local toy and craft shops, including spinning tops and an obstacle game called *jouet de la grenouille* (literally, "frog game") played in Normandy since the Middle Ages.

7 Glassware
The glassworks in the Bresle Valley are renowned, accounting for 80 per cent of luxury perfume bottles. The Musée des Traditions Verrières in Eu displays examples of astonishing beauty, while at the 16th-century Manoir de Fontaine in Blangy-sur-Bresle, you can watch weekend glass-blowing demonstrations and buy examples of the art.

8 Copper
A warm, burnished glow emanates from shop windows crammed with copper pots and pans in picturesque Villedieu-les-Pôeles. Copper has been its business since the 12th century, reaching a peak in the mid-18th, when there were nearly 150 workshops in town. Today, there is no better place to buy copper utensils (*poêles* means pots) or to see the craftsmen at work *(see p99).*

9 Dovecotes
Until the French Revolution, only wealthy landowners had the right to keep pigeons, and the size of the dovecote (*colombier*) was a mark of prosperity. Look out for Normandy's many fine examples, mellow with age: circular, square or polygonal, tiled and half-timbered, or patterned in brick and flint.

10 Arts and Crafts Outlets
Each July, there is an excellent arts and crafts fair, Le Festival de Métiers d'Art de Reviers, in Reviers (Calvados). In the Forêt de Brotonne (Eure), visit the Maison des Métiers at Bourneville, and the linen and clog-makers' workshops at Routot. Also keep an eye out for workshops in towns and villages, and arts and crafts on sale at markets and antiques fairs. The fair in Les Andelys in early September, for example, dates back to the Middle Ages.

Copper pans, Villedieu-les-Pôeles

Left **Forêt d'Eu** Right **Abbaye de la Trappe, Forêt du Perche**

TOP 10 Forests

1 Forêt d'Eawy
Although the name "Eawy" (pronounced "Ee-a-vee") means wet pasture, this is a glorious beech forest covering 72 sq km (28 sq miles) on a jagged outcrop. It was originally planted with oaks, which were subsequently cut down to build houses after the Hundred Years' War. To see other species, follow the Chemin des Écoliers.

2 Forêt de Reno-Valdieu
Walk or cycle along the path carved through the middle of the forest, and admire a magnificent line of giant oaks that soar up to 40 m (130 ft). They were planted in the 17th century, with beech trees, on the orders of Colbert, to make planks for naval ships.

3 Forêt d'Écouves
With its dense thickets of oak, beech and imported spruce and Scots pine covering the eastern end of the hills of Basse-Normandie, at 140 sq km (54 sq miles), this is the region's largest, wildest and arguably most beautiful forest. It supports a varied wildlife, including rare birds, deer and boar. Tucked away in Bois de Goult is a charming 11th-century chapel, frescoed with hunting scenes.

Tower of Bonvouloir, **Forêt des Andaines**

4 Forêt des Andaines
You might glimpse deer or roebuck roaming through the forest that encircles Bagnoles-de-l'Orne, and you will certainly see many different species of tree, including Japanese larch and Canadian fir. Try to visit the priory dedicated to St Ortaire, and the attractive observation tower of Bonvouloir.

5 Forêt de Lyons
This 100 sq km (37 sq mile) beech forest was a favourite hunting ground of Merovingian kings. Tall, slender beech trees cast a beautiful, dappled light, making it a perfect place for walking. As well as Lyons-la-Forêt (see pp63, 79), there are two châteaux and the ruined Abbaye de Mortemer to explore.

Forêt d'Écouves

Forêt d'Eu
6 This forest of beeches and many more exotic trees covers three large plateaux: Triage Forêt d'Eu, Haute Forêt d'Eu and Basse Forêt d'Eu. Among the highlights are a spectacular view of the Yères Valley from Poteau de Ste-Cathérine, and a pair of intertwined oak and beech trees, known as the *bonne entente* (happy couple).

Forêt de Brotonne
7 Heart of the Parc Naturel Régional des Boucles de la Seine Normande, this peaceful forest of towering oak, beech and pine, almost encircled by a loop in the Seine and reached by the soaring Brotonne Bridge, affords breathtaking views. It is home to deer, boar and hare, and in spring produces a carpet of bluebells.

Forêt du Perche et de la Trappe
8 Glimpse the characteristic *étangs* (pools) through the trees from the D603, which bisects these neighbouring forests, usually regarded as one. A ramble here might turn into a mushroom hunt: the ferny floor is a breeding ground for ceps and chanterelles. Don't miss Abbaye de la Trappe, home to Trappist monks.

Forêt de Belleme
9 Like the Forêt du Perche et de la Trappe,

Forêt de Belleme

this forest is dotted with pools, including the lovely Étang de la Herse. Of its many splendid oak trees, the most famous is the Chêne de l'École on the western fringes – 40 m (130 ft) tall and more than 300 years old.

Forêt de Roumare
10 With the Forêts de Rouvray, Verte and La Londe, this forest forms a 140 sq km (50 sq mile) crown around Rouen. Children will enjoy watching the roe and fallow deer

Wild boar, Forêt de Roumare

and wild boar in the Parc Animalier (wildlife park) near Canteleu on its eastern border, where there is also a 15th-century subterranean convent in the caves of Ste-Barbe.

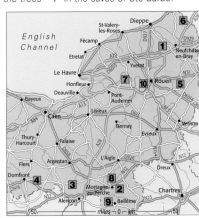

For more on regional natural parks **See pp42–43**

Left **Musée du Chemin de Fer Miniature** Right **Ludiver Observatory, Cap de la Hague**

 Activities for Children

1 Village Enchanté
A miniature train whisks you around the stunning park that forms the setting for this fantasy village. Enchanted waterfalls, a valley of fairy tales and puppet shows are aimed at the under-12s. ◈ *Bellefontaine • Map C5 • Open early Apr–end Oct: daily; phone 02 33 59 01 93 to check times • www.village-enchante.fr • Adm charge*

2 Parc Zoologique Cerzä
To call Cerzä a zoo is to do it a disservice. More than 50 hectares (123 acres) have been set aside to provide a natural environment for animals – tigers, lemurs, many African and endangered species. It also oversees breeding programmes. ◈ *Hermival-les-Vaux • Map F4 • 02 31 62 15 76 • Open Feb–Mar, Oct–Nov: 10am–5:30pm daily; Apr–Jun, Sep: 9:30am–6:30pm daily; Jul–Aug: 9:30am–7pm daily • www.cerza.com • Adm charge*

Festyland

3 Festyland
Amusement park for children of all ages, with a roller coaster, bouncy castles, water slides, go-karts and a circus on summer afternoons. ◈ *Caen-Carpiquet • Map D3 • 02 31 75 04 04 • Open Apr–mid-Jun: 11am–6pm Wed, Sat, Sun and national holidays; last 2 weeks Jun: 1:30–6pm; Jul–Aug: 10am–7pm daily • Adm charge*

4 Natur'Aquarium de Trouville
Trouville's famous beachside aquarium has an ecological bias, with recreated habitats such as mangrove swamps and rainforests. ◈ *Trouville • Map E3 • 02 31 88 46 04 • Open Easter–Jun, Sep–Oct: 10am–noon, 2–6pm daily; Jul–Aug: 10am–6pm daily; Nov–Easter: 2–6pm daily • Adm charge*

5 Parc de Loisirs L'Ange Michel
Quad bikes, trampolines, dry-slope sledges, bumper boats, "Aqua-splash" (small boats that whizz down long slides) and plenty more will keep the children happy for hours. ◈ *St-Martin-de-Landelles • Map C5 • 02 33 49 04 74 • Open mid-Apr–May, Sep: 11am–6pm Sat–Sun, bank hols; Jun: 10:30am–6pm daily; Jul–Aug: 10:30am–7pm daily • Adm charge*

6 Vélo Rail Experience
Ride a pedal-powered "bicycle train" and take in the scenery along disused railway lines in the Orne and Noireau river valleys. ◈ *Between Caen and Flers • Map D4 • 02 31 69 39 30 • www.rails-suissenormande.fr • Open Apr–Oct • Adm*

7 Musée du Chemin de Fer Miniature

One of Europe's largest model railways. ☀ Clécy • Map D4 • Open Mar–Easter: 2–5:30pm Sun; Easter–Jun: 10am–noon, 2–6 pm daily; Jul–Aug: 10am–noon, 2–6:30pm daily; Sep: 10am–12:30pm Tue–Fri, 10am–7pm Sat; Oct–Nov: 2–5pm Sun • Adm charge

8 Alligator Bay

Meet snakes, lizards, crocodiles and tortoises. ☀ Beauvoir • Map B5 • 02 33 68 11 18 • Open Apr–Sep: 10am–7pm daily; Oct–Mar: 2–6pm daily • Adm charge

Live exhibit at Alligator Bay

9 Ludiver, Cap de la Hague

A fascinating day out for young scientists, Ludiver is an observatory, planetarium and meteorology station. Among the treats on offer are a 3-D trek through the solar system, a journey to the centre of the earth, and a chance to view images from the main (600mm) telescope, either directly or in an indoor amphitheatre. ☀ Flottemanville-Hague • Map A2 • Open Jul–Aug: 10am–7pm daily; Sep–Jun: 9am–12:30pm, 2–5:30pm Mon–Fri, 2–6pm Sun • Adm charge

10 Artmazia

Find your way through the world's longest maze, made up of 5,000 beech and hornbeam trees. The park also has orchards and an art garden. ☀ Massy • Map J2 • 02 35 93 17 12 • Open May–Aug: 2:30–6:30pm daily; Sep: 2:30–6:30pm Sat & Sun; some eves in Aug–Sep • Adm charge

Top 10 Tips for Families

1 Restaurants
Most are child-friendly, have highchairs and offer an inexpensive menu d'enfants.

2 Picnics
A fun way to feed the family without having to worry about the mess. Pack picnic equipment and shop at local markets.

3 Hotels
In most hotels, children under 12 can sleep in a bed in their parents' room at little or no extra cost.

4 Gîtes
If you can't face a hotel, consider renting a house (see p133).

5 Car Travel
If you're hiring, book child seats in advance. Stock up with water, food and games before journeys.

6 Trains
Under-4s travel free; 4-to-12s, half-price.

7 Tourist Trains
A painless way to see the sights, these trains run through various town centres. Details from tourist offices.

8 River Trips
Organized trips with unique views of the countryside include ones on the Douve and Taute in Cotentin (see p117).

9 Farms
Pet the animals and see country life at close quarters at farms throughout Normandy. Check with tourist offices.

10 Sightseeing
Children under 6 can visit many sights free; tickets for under-12s are usually reduced-price.

Left **Golf, Omaha Beach** Right **Bungee jumping, Souleuvre Viaduct**

Outdoor Activities

1 Golf
Golfers are spoilt for choice in Normandy, which has 37 courses – 23 of them with 18 holes or more. Notable ones include Golf d'Étretat, situated on the clifftop above the famous Falaise d'Aval *(see p78)*, and Golf de Saint-Saëns, with beautiful views over the Forêt d'Eawy *(see p66)*. Deauville has no less than three top courses, and there are fine 27-hole courses at Omaha Beach and Granville.

2 Cycling
Cycling is the best way to take in the glorious Norman countryside. Each *département* has marked cycle routes, with accompanying booklets available from tourist offices. In Manche, old railway lines and towpaths are being turned into cycle paths. The forests of Lyons and Brotonne and the Eure and Seine Valleys are all excellent cycling areas.

3 Mountain Biking
The Perche is particularly suited to mountain biking, with marked trails at various levels of difficulty (maps available from Mortagne-au-Perche and Domfront tourist offices). The terrain is also suitable in the Suisse Normande and at Amayé-sur-l'Orne.

4 Walking and Rambling
Normandy is wonderful walking country. Official footpaths (marked by red-and-white posts) criss-cross the region, while the National Hiking Trails (Grandes Randonnées, or GR) provide spectacular long-distance routes. These include the GR23 (Seine and Forêt de Brotonne), GR223 (Cotentin Peninsula coast), and GR221 (Suisse Normande).

5 Bungee Jumping
At the now defunct Souleuvre railway viaduct (built in 1889 by Gustave Eiffel), apparently sane people choose to dive toward the ground secured by an elastic rope around the ankles, or scoot across the valley at 60 mph (100 kph) in a harness suspended from a cable. ◉ *Map C4 • AJ Hackett Bungy: 02 31 66 31 66 (reservations required)*

Horse riding, Village du Cheval, St-Michel-des-Andaines

6 Horse Riding
Normandy has many equestrian centres – especially in the Orne, where, for example, Le Village du Cheval in St-Michel-des-Andaines offers a wide variety of horsey activities. You can take a full-blown trekking holiday or just a few hours' ride *(see p117)*.

There are cycle-hire outlets across Normandy, and free transport for bicycles on trains.

7 Sand Yachting and Watersports

Normandy's broad, sandy beaches lend themselves perfectly to sand yachting (*char à voile*), particularly at Omaha Beach and along the west coast of the Cotentin Peninsula (there are large centres at Vauville and Portbail). You will also find windsurfing on offer, and something called "kitesurfing" (imagine snowboarding on water, wearing a harness with a kite attached). Sailors can choose from the 100 sailing schools and clubs along the coastline.

Canoeing

8 Canoeing

Condé-sur-Vire is Normandy's largest canoeing and kayaking resort; the Vire makes a perfect family outing (*see p98*). Canoeing is also on offer at Pont d'Ouilly in the Suisse Normande, on the Eure near Pacy-sur-Eure, and at Saint-Saëns in the Pays de Bray.

9 Fishing

The marvellous diversity of Norman lakes and rivers makes freshwater fishing a rewarding and popular pastime. Sea fishing expeditions are organized from ports including Honfleur, Trouville, Dieppe and St-Valéry-en-Caux.

10 Bases de Loisirs

Normandy has many *base de loisirs* (leisure bases) by lakes and on rivers, where you can enjoy swimming and watersports. Many also offer tennis, golf, riding, archery and other facilities.

Top 10 Walks

1 La Hague Peninsula

The coastal path GR223 passes the dramatic Nez de Jobourg (*see pp97, 101*).

2 Val de Saire

This pastoral valley makes gentle walking country. Finish at St-Vaast-la-Hougue or at Barfleur (*see pp100, 101*).

3 Dunes and Marshes, Bréhal

Take the *route submersible* to see one of Cotentin's unique natural havens, Havre de la Vanlée – but be warned, the road becomes heavily flooded during the dramatic spring tides. ❧ *Map B4*

4 Waterfalls of Mortain

Follow the river Cance, in an Alpine landscape. ❧ *Map C5*

5 La Suisse Normande

Rugged walking country, with great views from the Roche d'Oëtre (*see p88*).

6 Pays d'Auge

Rolling pastures, pretty villages, and plenty of stops for cheese and cider (*see pp32–3*).

7 Forêt du Perche et de la Trappe

Combine walking with mushrooming amidst woods and pools of water (*see p67*).

8 L'Aigle

Market day (Tuesday) is the best day for a walking tour of this historic town and its neighbouring cantons (*see p110*).

9 Forêt d'Eawy

Explore one of Normandy's most beautiful beech forests by walking the Chemin des Écoliers (*see p66*).

10 The Seine

Follow the GR23 along the Seine's south bank and into the Forêt de Brotonne (*see p67*).

There are good *bases de loisirs* at Lac de Caniel (Seine-Maritime), Léry-Poses (Eure), and Escale de Vitou in Vimoutiers (Orne).

Left **L'Armada, Rouen** Right **Festival du Cinéma Américain, Deauville**

Festivals and Events

1 Carnaval de Granville

The Carnaval de Granville began in the 16th century as a farewell party for local fishermen. Today, people flock from all over France to see the extravagantly decorated floats at this four-day event, which starts on the Sunday before Shrove Tuesday. On the last day, family members and friends disguise themselves behind masks and surprise each other. ◉ *Map B5 • Granville tourist office: 02 33 91 30 03*

2 Foire au Boudin, Mortagne-au-Perche

For 40 years, a fair has been held in Mortagne-au-Perche halfway through Lent to celebrate the local gourmet speciality *boudin noir*, a long sausage made from pig's blood, onions and pork fat.

Jazz sous les Pommiers, Coutances

Over three days, butchers gather to sell more than 5 km (3 miles) of this delicacy. Competitions include one to find the person who can eat the most. ◉ *Map H6 • Mortagne tourist office: 02 33 85 11 18*

3 Jazz sous les Pommiers, Coutances

Jazz sous les Pommiers (Jazz under the Apple Trees) has now been running for more than 20 years, and each year it grows in size and cachet. Over one week in May, it features concerts by established artists, as well as showcasing new talent. There are also promenade concerts, street performances and jam sessions. ◉ *Map B4 • Coutances tourist office: 02 33 19 08 10 • www. jazzsouslespommiers.com*

Foire au Boudin, Mortagne-au-Perche

For more culinary specialities **See pp54–5**

Fête des Marins, Honfleur

4 Local fishing boats, specially decorated for the occasion, meet in the Vieux Bassin on Whit Sunday to start their parade, which finishes with a priest's blessing in the Seine estuary. The festival continues the next day when fishermen and sailors process with model ships to Chapelle Notre-Dame de Grâce. ◈ *Map F3 • Honfleur tourist office: 02 31 89 23 30*

L'Armada, Rouen

5 In late June/early July every four or five years, Rouen hosts a fleet of tall ships and battleships from across the globe. The city and its environs buzz with festivities and firework displays for eight lively days and nights, culminating in a colourful parade of boats down the Seine. The next Armada takes place in 2013. ◈ *Map J3 • www.armada.org*

Pèlerinage d'Eté au Mont-St-Michel

6 A crossing of the sands from Genêts to Mont-St-Michel every July perpetuates the tradition of the great pilgrimages of the Middle Ages. It attracts about 1,500 "pilgrims". ◈ *Map B5 • Presbytère de Sartilly: 02 33 48 80 37*

Le Normandy Horse Show à St-Lô

7 This major event in the equestrian calendar takes place over one week in August, and includes auctions of horses, ponies and donkeys, as well as numerous competitions; the showjumping and obstacle courses are among the favourites. Spectators will see all sorts of different breeds, from sporting to cart horses. ◈ *Map C4 • Centre de Promotion de l'Élevage, Haras National, ave du Maréchal-Juin: 02 33 77 88 66*

Foire de Sainte-Croix, Lessay

8 The date of the first Holy Cross Fair is lost in the mists of time, but it was probably in the 11th century and supported by Benedictine monks. In the 21st century, some 400,000 people gather over three days on the second weekend in September. As well as almost 2,000 exhibitors and livestock sales, there are carnival rides and traditional spit roasts. ◈ *Map B3 • Lessay tourist office: 02 33 45 14 34*

Foire de Sainte-Croix, Lessay

Festival du Cinéma Américain, Deauville

9 Even though it is not quite as prestigious as Cannes or Venice, this festival dedicated to the best American movies of the year always attracts its share of Hollywood stars. Unsurprisingly, the premières are the most popular screenings. Awards are given by an all-French jury. ◈ *Map E3 • Deauville tourist office: 02 31 14 40 00 • www.festival-deauville.com*

Foire aux Dindes, Sées

10 On the second Saturday in December, the seductive medieval town of Sées is filled with the sound of gobbling. People come from all over Orne and beyond to Normandy's largest and most important turkey fair to preview their Christmas dinner. ◈ *Map E5 • Sées tourist office: 02 33 28 74 79*

Following pages **Château St-Germain-de-Livet, Pays d'Auge**

AROUND NORMANDY

NORMANDY'S TOP 10

Left **Water lilies at Giverny** Right **Côte d'Albâtre coastline**

Northeastern Normandy

INLAND FROM THE DRAMATIC CÔTE D'ALBÂTRE, with its harbours and seaside resorts sheltering between chalky cliffs, northeastern Normandy is dominated by the Seine, which follows a meandering course at its southern border. An unspoilt region of forests and rivers, it embraces the département of Seine-Maritime – north of the Seine and reaching to the Epte – a slice of Eure. At the confluence of the two rivers is Giverny, the village made famous by Monet. Seine-Maritime has a varied landscape with the lush, sparsely populated Pays de Bray in the northeast and, at its heart, the limestone plateau of the Pays de Caux. Between the sea and the cultured cathedral city of Rouen, one magnificent abbey after another overlooks the wooded banks of the Seine Valley – stations on the well-trodden Abbey Route.

Rouen

Rouen

1 Founded by the Romans around 50 BC, the capital of Haute-Normandie occupied a strategic site on the Seine – the last point where the river could be bridged. From the end of the Hundred Years' War, when the French retook the city from the English, Rouen prospered through textile production and maritime trade. In the 20th century, industry expanded on the south bank. The north bank's many treasures – including streets of half-timbered houses and the magnificent cathedral – attract thousands of visitors every year *(see pp20–23)*.

Abbaye de Jumièges

2 The breathtakingly lovely ruins of a 7th-century abbey, which once housed a community of 900 monks *(see pp18–19)*.

Giverny

3 Pay homage to Monet in his own home – now the Fondation Claude Monet – and wander in the gardens that inspired him. The Musée des Impressionnismes explores the history of Impressionism, post-Impressionism and the movement's influence on 20th-century art *(see pp34–7)*.

Dieppe

4 The first beach resort in France, Dieppe occupies a striking position between limestone cliffs. As a Channel port, it was coveted for centuries by foreign invaders, and has long been a favourite with British holiday-makers, drawn by its sweeping beach and lively old town centred on the Grande Rue *(see p58)*. Nearby, medieval Église St-Jacques has a memorial to the thousands of Canadians killed in Operation Jubilee in 1942. Above the town, the 15th-century flint-

View of Dieppe from Chateau

and-sandstone castle is now a museum, with a fine collection of Impressionists and some remarkable 16th-century carved ivory pieces. ◈ *Map J1 • Tourist office: pont Jehan Ango, quai du Carénage. 02 32 14 40 60*

Le Havre

5 Le Havre was founded in 1517 to replace the ports of Honfleur, Harfleur and Caudebec, which had silted up. Now it is the country's second port and a UNESCO World Heritage site, a tribute to its recovery from the bombing raids that flattened it in 1944. One of the few survivors is the 16th-century Cathédrale Notre-Dame, an architectural hybrid of Gothic and Renaissance styles, bristling with gargoyles. The city was rebuilt to designs by Auguste Perret, with reinforced concrete as the main material. Typical of his style is the starkly imposing Église St-Joseph. More modern is the building of glass, aluminium and steel housing the Musée Malraux *(see p53)*. In the suburb of Montivilliers is the Abbaye Notre-Dame, a Benedictine abbey for women. ◈ *Map E2 • Tourist office: 186 blvd Clémenceau. 02 32 74 04 04*

The Seine

The second-longest, busiest and most famous river in France, the Seine has its source in Burgundy, flows through Paris, and finally meets the sea at Le Havre. Its lower course through Normandy is wide enough to accommodate large ships and barges – hence its historical importance for settlers and invaders, and the location of Rouen and the Norman abbeys.

6 Côte d'Albâtre

On first sight of the Alabaster Coast, you might be fooled into thinking that you were across the Channel: it bears a striking resemblance to the White Cliffs of Dover. Stretching southwest from Le Tréport to Le Havre, the coastline is pitted by *valleuses* – dry hanging valleys in the clifftops, revealed as the cliffs retreat before the combined forces of sea and weather. The harbours shelter in natural shingle inlets, while the larger towns cluster on the estuaries. This coast offers some of the region's most spectacular scenery. ◈ *Map E2, G2, H1, J1*

7 Étretat

Nestling between two cliffs, Falaises d'Aval and d'Amont, this picturesque village was a sleepy place until the 19th-century onslaught of writers, painters and Parisian holiday-makers. For the best view of Falaise d'Aval – an extraordinary rock formation with a natural arch, which Maupassant likened to an elephant dipping its trunk into the sea – climb to Notre-Dame-de-la-Garde, the chapel on top of Falaise d'Amont. Nearby, a museum and monument commemorate aviators Nungesser and Colia, whose aeroplane was last seen near here on the first, failed attempt to fly the Atlantic in 1927. In Étretat itself, visit the place du Maréchal-Foch, where 16th-century houses cluster around timbered *halles* – an attractive 1920s reconstruction of a wooden covered market. ◈ *Map G2 • Tourist office: pl Maurice Guillard. 02 35 27 05 21*

8 Fécamp

After a casket said to contain precious drops of Christ's blood was washed ashore in the first century, Fécamp became a pilgrimage centre. First an abbey (now ruined) was built to house the holy relic, then the glorious 12th- to 13th-century Abbatiale de la Trinité *(see p47)*. More prosaically, the cornerstone of this no-nonsense fishing port was the humble cod, as a trip to the Musée des Terra Neuvas et de la Pêche proves. Fécamp's other claim to fame is Bénédictine, first made in 1863 by merchant Alexandre le Grand from an old monastic recipe. It continues to be distilled in his overblown 19th-century Palais Bénédictine, which contains laboratories, museum and gallery, and offers tastings *(see p82)*. ◈ *Map G2 • Tourist office: quai Sadi-Carnot. 02 35 28 51 01*

Falaise d'Aval

For more on Étretat **See p60**

Chateau Gaillard and Les Andelys

9 Les Andelys and Château Gaillard

The twin villages of Grand and Petit Andelys enjoy a glorious setting on a lazy curve of the Seine in the shadow of the pale ruins of Richard the Lionheart's Château Gaillard, built at breakneck speed in 1196 to prevent Philippe Auguste from reaching Rouen. Below lie the winding streets of tranquil, timbered Petit Andely, and more commercial Grand Andely, with a fine 16th- to 17th-century church and two interesting museums – one dedicated to the painter Nicolas Poussin, the other to the Normandie-Niémen regiment.
Ⓢ Map J3 • Tourist office: rue Philippe Auguste. 02 32 54 41 93

10 Lyons-la-Forêt

Visit this picture-postcard town in the Lieure Valley and you'll understand why Ravel used to come here to compose. Sights nearby include the impressive, early-17th-century pink-brick Château de Fleury-la-Forêt, with a superb collection of toys and dolls; Château de Vascoeuil, which has traditional cottages and modern sculpture in its grounds; and the ruined Cistercian Abbaye de Mortemer with its museum.
Ⓢ Map K2 • Tourist office: 20 rue de l'Hôtel de Ville. 02 32 49 31 65

A Drive through the Val de Seine

Morning

🕐 Take the D982 from Rouen to St-Martin-de-Boscherville to visit the lovely Romanesque abbey of **St-Georges de Boscherville** (see p80). Walk around the gardens and enjoy the views. After a browse in the abbey shop, revive yourself at one of the village bars.

Continue on the D982 until you reach the D143 turn-off for the bewitching, ruined **Abbaye de Jumièges** (see pp18–19). This is a place for calm contemplation, so don't rush your visit. Afterwards, make your way to the picturesque Seine-side inn **Auberge du Bac** (2 rue Alphonse Callais) for lunch.

Afternoon

Retrace your steps to the D982 and head on to the **Abbaye de St-Wandrille** (see p80). Finish with a visit to the shop, filled with goods produced by the monks.

Cross the elegant **Pont de Brotonne** into the **Forêt de Brotonne** (see p67) via the D40, and spend the rest of the afternoon exploring this tranquil forest at the heart of the **Parc Régional Naturel des Boucles de la Seine Normande** (see p42). Visit the **Maison du Parc** in Notre-Dame-de-Bliquetuit, then stop for tea at the simple **Chez Agnès**. Leave the forest on the D913, take the little roads via Barneville and Mauny to **La Bouille**, where the bac (ferryboat) will ferry you across the river to Sahurs. From here, turn right and follow signs for Rouen.

For more on Lyons-la-Forêt **See p63**

Left **Caudebec-en-Caux** Right **Abbaye de St-Wandrille**

🔟 Best of the Rest

1 Caudebec-en-Caux
A jaunty Seine-side town with a centuries-old Saturday market, museum of river life, Flamboyant Gothic church and medieval Templar's house. ◈ *Map H2 • Tourist office: pl du Général de Gaulle. 02 32 70 46 32*

2 Gisors
In the capital of Norman Vexin, a fine 13th- to 14th-century church keeps company with the castle William the Conqueror built to protect his borders. ◈ *Map K3 • Tourist office: 4 rue du Général de Gaulle. 02 32 27 60 63*

3 Le Tréport
This popular seaside town is famous for its smoked fish *(see p82)* – also for the view of the coast from the Calvaire (calvary) above the town. ◈ *Map J1 • Tourist office: quai Sadi Carnot. 02 35 86 05 69*

4 Villequier
At a beautiful spot on the Seine, Villequier marks the point where river becomes estuary. Victor Hugo's daughter Léopoldine drowned here in 1843. The Musée Victor-Hugo commemorates her life. ◈ *Map H2 • Musée Victor-Hugo: Open 10am–12:30pm, 2–5:30pm Mon, Wed–Sat, 2–5:30pm Sun. Adm charge*

5 Abbaye St-Georges de Boscherville
An exquisite example of Norman Romanesque architecture. ◈ *St-Martin-de-Boscherville • Map H3 • Open Apr–Oct: 9am–6:30pm daily; Nov–Mar: 2–5pm daily. Adm charge*

6 Abbaye de St-Wandrille
The chequered history of this working Benedictine monastery goes back to 649, and includes a spell in the 19th century as home to the Marquis of Stackpole. ◈ *Map H2 • Guided tours: phone 02 35 96 23 11 for details*

7 Eu
The handsome collegiate church in this tranquil riverside town is named after the Irish primate St Lawrence, who died here in 1180 *(see p81)*. ◈ *Map J1 • Tourist office: pl Guillaume le Conquérant. 02 35 86 04 68*

8 Varengeville-sur-Mer
Gloriously situated, its cliff-top church has windows by Ubac and Braques. Lutyens and Gertrude Jekyll collaborated on the nearby Parc du Bois des Moutiers *(see p45)*. ◈ *Map J1*

9 Écouis
The heart of Écouis is the church of Notre-Dame, built by Enguerrand de Marigny in 1313. The ruined 12th-century Abbaye de Fontaine Guérard is worth a short excursion. ◈ *Map K3 • Abbaye de Fontaine Guérard: Fleury-sur-Andelle. Open Apr–Oct: pm Tue–Sun. Adm charge*

10 Veules-les-Roses
In its own valley, at the mouth of the shortest river in France, this pretty village clusters round its 12th-century church. ◈ *Map H1 • Tourist office: 27 rue Victor Hugo. 02 35 97 63 05*

Left **Manoir d'Ango** Right **Château de Filières**

₁₀ Châteaux

1 Château de Miromesnil
Visit the Montebello salon and the Marquis de Miromesnil's rooms in the 16th- to 17th-century mansion where Maupassant was born. ◈ *Tourville-sur-Arques • Map J1 • Apr–Nov: 2–6pm Wed–Mon (Jun–Aug: 10am–1pm, 2–6pm daily) • Adm charge*

2 Château d'Eu
Queen Victoria came to stay in Louis Philippe's 16th-century holiday home, now the Musée Louis-Philippe, crammed with antiques. ◈ *Eu • Map J1 • Open mid-Mar–Oct: 10am–noon, 2–6pm Wed–Mon (Fri pm only) • Adm charge*

3 Manoir d'Ango
A glorious Italian Renaissance manor, built in the early 16th century. ◈ *Varengeville-sur-Mer • Map J1 • 02 35 83 61 56 • Open Easter–end Sep: 10am–12:30pm, 2–6pm daily; Oct: Sat, Sun & public hols • Adm charge*

4 Château de Vascoeuil
This stately home has a grand courtyard and exceptional dovecote. The grounds feature over 50 sculptures. ◈ *Vascoeuil • Map J3 • 02 35 23 62 35 • Open Apr–Nov: 2:30–6pm Wed–Sun (Jul, Aug: 10:30am–6:30pm daily) • Adm charge*

5 Château d'Orcher
This 11th-century fort (remodelled in the 18th century) has a spectacular clifftop setting and a park with avenues of ash. ◈ *Gonfreville l'Orcher • Map G2 • 02 35 45 45 91 • Open 1 Jul–15 Aug: 2–6pm Tue–Sun • Adm charge*

6 Château de Filières
The left wing is all that remains of the original Henri IV house. The park's vaulted beech avenue is known as La Cathédrale. ◈ *Gommerville • Map G2 • 02 35 20 53 30 • Open 1 May–1 Oct: pm Wed, Sat, Sun & public hols (Jul–Aug: daily) • Adm charge*

7 Château d'Ételan
A striking example of the 15th-century Flamboyant Gothic, this château – in two parts linked by a stone staircase – has a jewel of a chapel. ◈ *St-Maurice-d'Ételan • Map H3 • 02 35 39 91 27 • Open mid-Jun–Sep: 3–7pm daily • Adm charge*

8 Château de Cany-Barville
This impressive moated château of stone and brick, built by François Mansart (whose uncle built Versailles) in the 1640s, has always been in the same family. ◈ *Cany • Map H2 • Open Jul–Aug: 10am–noon, 3–6pm Sat–Thu • Adm charge*

9 Château de Galleville
The former home of Maréchal de Villars, this late-1600s château displays a rare consistency of architectural style. ◈ *Doudeville • Map H2 • 02 35 96 54 65 • Open 22 Jul–31 Aug: 2–6pm daily • Adm charge*

10 Château du Mesnil-Geoffroy
This 17th-century house of brick and stone has a large garden with a hornbeam maze by Le Nôtre gardener Colinet. ◈ *Ermenouville • Map H1 • 02 35 57 12 77 • Open May–Sep: Fri–Sun pm, hols • Adm charge*

Left **Monk, Abbaye de St-Wandrille** Right **Monique de St-Romaine**

🔟 Places to Shop

1 Abbaye de St-Wandrille
A 14th-century barn houses the abbey shop, outlet for the monks' own products, including CDs of Gregorian chant, honey and beeswax candles. ◈ *Map H2*

2 Faïencerie Augy, Rouen
Attractive plates, jugs, vases and lamps are decorated and fired according to 16th-century methods in the workshops attached to this seductive faïence shop. Demonstrations by appointment. ◈ *26 rue St-Romain • Map M5 • 02 35 88 77 47*

3 Monique de St-Romaine, Rouen
Going to a wedding or the races at Deauville? Get a one-off hat at this charming, old-fashioned *modiste* (milliner), the city's sole survivor. ◈ *58 rue St-Romain • Map M5*

4 Palais Bénédictine, Fécamp
Taste the liqueur, aged in casks in the palace basement, before visiting the shop, well stocked with Bénédictines and B&B (Bénédictine blended with brandy). ◈ *110 rue Alexandre-Le-Grand • Map G2 • Closed Jan–early Feb*

5 Delgove et Cie, Le Tréport
Following this area's traditional method of smoking fish (drying in sawdust before smoking over a beechwood fire), this smoke-house sells salmon, mackerel, herring and haddock. ◈ *Parc Sainte-Croix • Map J1*

6 Aux Deux Gouttes d'Eau, Forges-les-Eaux
Alexandre Audel is a potter from Martinique specializing in Vieux-Forges faïence. He also takes commissions. ◈ *pl de l'Ancienne Gare • Map K2*

7 L'Epicier Olivier, Dieppe
Every kind of French gourmet product is stocked here: charcuterie and cheeses, fine coffees, mustards, preserves and a magnificent selection of fine wines, ciders and liqueurs. ◈ *18 rue St-Jacques • Map J1 • 02 35 84 22 55 • Open Tue–Sat (Jul & Aug: also Mon pm)*

8 Caves Bérigny, Rouen
French wines and the best Normandy ciders and Calvados line the shelves at this attractive shop. There are also branches in Fécamp, Lillebonne and Le Havre. ◈ *7 rue Rollon • Map J3 • 02 35 07 57 54 • Open Tue–Sat & Sun am*

9 Maison du Lin, Routot
Learn about the history and production of linen at this museum, then treat yourself to some napkins or a tea towel from the tempting shop. ◈ *pl du Général-Leclerc • Map H3 • 02 32 56 21 76 • Open mid-Mar–mid-Oct: daily*

10 Saveur Chocolat, Le Havre
The Auzou family have been *chocolatiers* since 1961. Their shop is the place to buy the famous "Tears of Joan of Arc" (chocolate-covered almonds). ◈ *19 rue Albert André-Huet • Map E2*

Price Categories

For a three course meal for one with half a bottle of wine (or equivalent meal), taxes and extra charges.	€ under €30
	€€ €30–€40
	€€€ €40–€50
	€€€€ €50–€60
	€€€€€ over €60

Au Souper Fin

Places to Eat

1 Le Vieux Carré, Rouen
Part of a boutique hotel, this popular *salon de thé* serves imaginative salads, tarts and sandwiches. The ideal spot for a light lunch. ⊗ *34 rue Ganterie • Map J3 • 02 35 71 67 70 • Closed D • €*

2 Domaine St-Clair, Étretat
Dine by candle-light at this elegant restaurant housed in a dramatically located seaside hotel. Chef Wilfrid Chaplain offers three fixed-price menus in addition to a good selection of à la carte dishes. ⊗ *chemin de St-Clair • Map G2 • 02 35 27 08 23 • €€€€*

3 Au Souper Fin, Frichemesnil
This snug restaurant in the village of Frichemesnil is the place to sample Eric Buisset's inventive, Michelin-starred cooking. ⊗ *1 rte de Clères • Map J2 • 02 35 33 33 88 • Closed Sun D, Wed, Thu • €€€*

4 La Licorne Royale, Lyons-la-Forêt
The restaurant of the Hôtel de la Licorne showcases the refined creative cuisine of Michelin-starred chef Christophe Poirier. ⊗ *27 pl Benserade • Map K3 • 02 32 48 24 24 • Closed Mon–Fri L • €€€€*

5 Bistrot du Pollet, Dieppe
Slightly out of the way – and all the better for it – this small, pretty bistro can put fish on your table within minutes of its being landed. ⊗ *23 rue Tête-de-Boeuf • Map J1 • 02 35 84 68 57 • Closed Sun–Mon • €*

6 Les Comptoirs de l'Océan, Le Tréport
This quayside restaurant wins the local vote with superb fish-based dishes and impeccable service. ⊗ *46 quai François 1er • Map J1 • 02 35 86 24 92 • €€*

7 Le Manoir de Rétival, Caudebec en Caux
German chef David Görne offers a different contemporary tasting menu every day. Booking required. ⊗ *2 rue St-Clair • Map F3 • 02 35 95 86 18 • €€€€€*

8 Ancien Hôtel Baudy, Giverny
Classic bistro lunches make a great accompaniment to any visit to Monet's garden. ⊗ *81 rue Claude Monet • Map K4 • 02 32 21 10 03 • Closed Mon D, Nov–Mar • €*

9 Le Moulin de Fourges, Fourges
A pretty mill on the bank of the Epte, offering memorable regional cuisine in a great setting. Fresh produce, prepared with skill and imagination. ⊗ *38 rue du Moulin • Map K4 • 02 32 52 12 12 • Closed Jan, Mon • €€€*

10 La Closerie, Vieux Villez
Located in the grounds of the Château Corneille, La Closerie offers regional specialities, a wide range of wines and two creative set menus based on local ingredients such as crab and lamb. ⊗ *17 rue de l'Église • Map J4 • 02 32 77 44 77 • €€*

Following pages **Beach at Deauville**

83

Left **Caen, historic centre** Right **The front at Deauville**

Central Normandy

ENCOMPASSING THE WHOLE OF THE *DÉPARTEMENT OF CALVADOS* and much of Eure, this region is the true heart of Normandy. From the earthly pleasures of Deauville to the heavenly aspirations of Ste-Thérèse's Lisieux, from the rural idyll of the Pays d'Auge to the architectural magnificence of the Château de Beaumesnil, from the Bayeux Tapestry to the Impressionist paintings inspired by the enchanting seaport of Honfleur, central Normandy is brimming with variety and interest. William the Conqueror – born in Falaise, buried in Caen – dominates the region's history, as do the events of D-Day, 6 June 1944, and the subsequent Battle of Normandy, played out on its wide, sandy beaches and in its attractive, historic and now carefully restored towns.

🔟 Sights

1. D-Day Beaches
2. Caen
3. Bayeux
4. Honfleur
5. Deauville and La Côte Fleurie
6. Pays d'Auge
7. Falaise
8. La Suisse Normande
9. Evreux
10. Vallée de l'Eure

St Catherine's quay, Honfleur

1 D-Day Beaches
Sixty years after D-Day, the momentous events of 6 June 1944, when the Allies landed on the beaches of the huge Seine Bay, are commemorated in memorials, museums and cemeteries (see pp28–31).

2 Caen
Reconstructed after the war, Caen retains its compact historic centre and Romanesque architectural masterpieces, including William the Conqueror's abbey church of St-Etienne, which sheltered hundreds of citizens during the ferocious Battle of Caen in 1944. Many visitors head straight for the absorbing Mémorial museum on the outskirts and then leave, but any time spent in this lively, cultured city with a fascinating history is time well spent (see pp24–5).

William and Harold, Bayeux Tapestry

3 Bayeux
Known the world over for its famous Tapestry, the small-scale, beautifully kept cathedral town itself is far less well known – yet full of charm. Allow two hours for a visit to the Tapestry in the Centre Guillaume-le-Conquérant, and at least another two to explore Vieux Bayeux (see pp12–15).

4 Honfleur
The highlight of Normandy's coast is this enchanting port, fortified during the Hundred Years' War and constantly fought over by the French and the English during that time. Today, it is celebrated both for the intrepid mariners who set sail from its harbour, and for the artists who found inspiration here. The special light of the Seine estuary is at its best, so the artists say, just after dawn (see pp16–17).

5 Deauville and La Côte Fleurie
Normandy's most alluring stretch of coast, fringed by marvellous sandy beaches, is enlivened by a string of resorts that offer some-thing for everyone: gambling or, if you can't afford to gamble, people-watching in opulent Deauville; shrimping and sand-yachting in Houlgate and Cabourg; and the many amusements of happy-go-lucky Trouville. The D513 follows the coast, dipping inland around the impressive corniche, Falaises des Vaches Noires, that rises up between Houlgate and Villers-sur-Mer (see pp26–7).

6 Pays d'Auge
If Normandy's long coastline reaches a peak of loveliness between Cabourg and Honfleur, then so does the landscape behind it. This is the Pays d'Auge, quint-essentially Norman countryside, rich in orchards and dairy produce, that stretches back from the Côte Fleurie and Côte de Grâce through the heart of the *département* of Calvados. Lisieux, famed for its connec-tions with Ste Thérèse, is its principal town, and there are many old manors and pretty villages to explore besides – as well as cheese, cider and Calvados to taste and buy (see pp32–3).

Calvados

The creation of Normandy's famous cider brandy is an art with many subtle variations. Look out on the label for VSOP (four years in the barrel), and Napoléon, Hors d'Age or Age Inconnu (at least five years in the barrel). Drink as a *digestif*, or follow French tradition and add a splash of *calva* to your coffee. If any excuse will do, knock back a *trou normand (see p55)*.

7 Falaise

The dashing equestrian statue of William the Conqueror, his charger rearing heroically, sets the tone in the main square of this attractive and intriguing town. Falaise is dominated by its vast fortress, Château Guillaume-le-Conquérant, birthplace of William in 1027. In August 1944, it was the site of the fierce and decisive Battle of the Mortain-Falaise Pocket. In the valley below, a modern sculpture recalls the spot where William's father, Robert the Magnificent, saw his future wife, the beautiful Arlette, washing clothes in the stream. Also worth a visit are Automates Avenue, a collection of 20th-century automata that once graced Parisian shop windows, and Musée Août 1944, housed in a former cheese factory. ⦿ *Map E4 • Tourist office: Le Forum, blvd de la Libération. 02 31 90 17 26*

8 La Suisse Normande

Hardly the Alps, but this popular, scenic region is as close to Switzerland as Normandy gets, and is very different from the typical Norman landscape. On its winding northwesterly course, the River Orne has cut through the *massif*,

creating steep banks and the occasional severe peak. The scenery along the valley is among Normandy's most striking. None of the "heights" are really that high, but they provide some dizzying views – and plenty of scope for outdoor pursuits. Many come for the canoeing, walking, fishing or rock-climbing; others come to hang-glide off the Pain de Sucre. Another high point is the craggy Roche d'Oëtre, with magnificent views over the Rouvre gorges and beyond. The principal tourist centres are Thury-Harcourt, Pont-d'Ouilly and Clécy *(see p90)*. ⦿ *Map D4, D5 • Tourist office: 2 pl St-Sauveur, Thury-Harcourt. 02 31 79 70 45*

9 Evreux

Capital of the *département* of Eure, Evreux has had a turbulent history and more than its fair share of siege and invasion since the Vandals first sacked it in the 5th century. Damaged during World War II, its centre has been rebuilt, and its gardens, footpaths and riverside walks make it a very pleasant town. In the Cathédrale de Notre-Dame, the Renaissance carvings round the north door date from the height of the Flamboyant period, as do the marvellously delicate leaf and flower motifs in the transept and the lantern tower. Despite

Swiss Normandy

Cathédrale de Notre-Dame, Evreux

fire and bombs, much of the antique glass has been restored. The Musée d'Evreux includes Gallo-Roman archaeological finds, plus fine carved misericords and tapestries in the medieval section. ◈ Map J4 • Tourist office: 1 pl. Général-de-Gaulle. 02 32 24 04 43

10 Vallée de l'Eure

Easily accessible from Paris, the lush Eure Valley is a popular weekend destination for city dwellers. The stretch of the Eure between Chartres and the Seine is sometimes referred to as the Valley of the Mistresses, since it passes first the château of Louis XIV's secret wife, Madame de Maintenon (just outside Normandy in Île de France), then Château d'Anet (see p91), commissioned by Diane de Poitiers, mistress of Henri II. From Anet, the D143 and D836 follow the river past attractive Ivry-la-Bataille and Pacy-sur-Eure, with its fine 13th-century church. A lovely stretch at Cocherel comes next, then Château d'Acquigny, set in a landscaped park. The Eure ends at Louviers, which has a small but pretty old quarter near its 13th-century church of Notre-Dame (see p92). ◈ Map J4 • Tourist office: pl. Dufay, Pacy-sur-Eure. 02 32 26 18 21

A Drive Along the Risle

Morning

🕐 Starting in **Pont-Audemer** (see p90), follow the sign-posted trail around the town's highlights. If it's Friday (market day), rue de la République will be lined with tempting food stalls.

Take the D130 for the lovely 24 km (15 mile) drive along the Risle and through the Fôret de Montfort to **Le Bec-Hellouin** (see p46). Wander in the abbey grounds and climb the Tour St-Nicolas for a fine view. The calm atmosphere of the village makes it a perfect setting for lunch. If you have a picnic, head back to Pont-Authou just north of Le Bec-Hellouin, and follow signs Canoe-Kayak-La Risle over a footbridge to a tranquil aire de pique-nique on an island in the river.

Afternoon

Leave Le Bec-Hellouin on the scenic D39 to St-Martin-du-Parc and Le Buhot, then turn left on the D26 to **Harcourt**, with its stern medieval fortress-château and the oldest arboretum in France (see p91). Leaving by the D137, reconnect with the Risle at **Brionne** (see p90). There's plenty to do here, including canoeing (see p93). The square keep (or donjon) on its hill is a fine sight against the setting sun; from it, there is a panoramic view over the Risle Valley. In town, there's a choice of cafés and restaurants for a relaxing evening drink or a meal. Best is the 18th-century **Auberge du Vieux Donjon** (rue Soie).

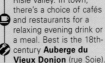

Left **Beaumont-le-Roger** Right **Pont-Audemer**

🔟 Country Towns

1 Bernay
It's worth penetrating the suburbs to find Bernay's share of picturesque timbered houses (among them rue Gaston-Follope, lined with antiques shops), an abbey church begun in 1013, and a handsome municipal museum. ◈ *Map H4 • Tourist office: 29 rue Thiers. 02 32 43 32 08*

2 Brionne
An excellent base for exploring the Risle Valley, this small market town is watched over by an 11th-century keep. ◈ *Map H3 • Tourist office: 1 rue du Général-de-Gaulle. 02 32 45 70 51*

3 Beaumont-le-Roger
The stark ruins of the 13th-century priory, and the parish church of St-Nicolas are eye-catching sights in this war-torn riverside town. ◈ *Map H4 • Tourist office: 1 pl de Clercq. 02 32 44 05 79*

4 Clécy
This pretty stone-built village in the Suisse Normande *(see pp42, 88)* boasts one of Europe's largest model railways *(see p69)*, but its main attraction is the wide range of holiday activities on offer. ◈ *Map D4 • Tourist office: pl du Tripot. 02 31 69 79 95*

5 Conches-en-Ouche
Approached on the D830 from Evreux, the town's fine setting above a bend in the River Rouloir is revealed. ◈ *Map H4 • Tourist office: pl Briand. 02 32 30 76 42*

6 Orbec
This delightful country town seems unconcerned about the tourist potential of its many fine old buildings, including the Vieux Manoir of 1563 in rue Grande. ◈ *Map G4 • Tourist office: 6 rue Grande. 02 31 32 56 68*

7 Pont-Audemer
In the charming town centre, encased like a jewel in its non-descript surroundings, water and half-timbered houses are the defining features. ◈ *Map G3 • Tourist office: pl Maubert. 02 32 41 08 21*

8 Pont-l'Eveque
This workaday Pays d'Auge town is famous for its cheese. Nearby, at Château de Betteville, the Belle Époque motor museum is worth a visit. ◈ *Map E3 • Tourist office: 16 bis pl Jean Bureau. 02 31 64 12 77*

9 Verneuil-sur-Avre
Chequered walls and turrets catch the eye in this fortified town on the old Franco-Norman border, as do the 13th-century Tour Grise and the striking tower of Ste-Madeleine *(see p92)*. ◈ *Map H5 • Tourist office: 129 pl de la Madeleine. 02 32 32 17 17*

10 Vernon
This smart residential town includes a former mill straddling two piers of a medieval bridge, the tiered Maison du Temps Jadis and the Tour des Archives, a castle keep *(see p92)*. ◈ *Map K4 • Tourist office: 36 rue Carnot. 02 32 51 39 60*

Left **Château de Beaumesnil** Right **Château de Fontaine-Henry**

🔟 Châteaux

1 Château d'Anet
Diane de Poitiers' once-fabulous château is now but a glimmer of its former glory, yet still impresses – especially the gatehouse with its amazing clock. ◈ Map K4 • 02 37 41 90 07 • Open Apr–Oct: pm Wed–Mon • Adm charge

2 Château de Balleroy
In the Waterloo Room of this sumptuous château, portraits of Napoleon and Wellington confront one another. A hot-air balloon museum is housed in the stables. ◈ Map C3 • 02 31 21 60 61 • Open Easter–Jun: pm Fri–Mon; Jul–Aug: daily; Sep: pm Wed–Mon • Adm charge

3 Château de Beaumesnil
This glorious Baroque master-piece, a frothy pile of pink brick and pale stone on a glassy moat, is perfectly complemented by the formal gardens that surround it. ◈ Map H4 • 02 32 44 40 09 • Open Easter–Jun, Sep–Oct: pm Fri–Mon; Jul, Aug: pm Wed–Mon • Adm charge

4 Château de Bénouville
The monumental staircase is the star at this impressive yet charming Neo-Classical château. ◈ Map D3 • 02 31 95 53 23 • Open Jul–Sep: pm Wed–Mon • Adm charge

5 Château de Bizy, Vernon
The interior of this handsome château set in an English-style park is graced by superb woodwork, tapestries and Empire furniture. ◈ blvd des Capucins • Map K4 • 02 32 51 00 82 • Open Apr–Oct: Tue–Sun • Adm charge

6 Château de Champ-de-Bataille, Le Neubourg
This soldierly 17th-century château is owned by interior design-er Jacques Garcia. On view are the kitchens, and lavish gardens inspired by mythology. ◈ Map H3 • Open Mar–Apr, Oct: weekends and hols; May–Sep pm daily (Jul–Aug: all day) • Adm charge

7 Château de Fontaine-Henry
The sloping roofs of this extraordinary Renaissance château are taller than its walls. ◈ Map D3 • 06 89 84 85 57 • Open Easter–mid-Jun, mid-Sep–Oct: pm Sat–Sun; mid-Jun–mid-Sep: pm Wed–Mon • Adm charge

8 Le Domaine d'Harcourt
The ancestral home of the Harcourt family has an important arboretum, created in 1802. ◈ Map H4 • 02 32 46 29 70 • Open mid-Jun–mid-Sep: daily; Mar–mid-Jun, mid-Sep–mid-Nov: pm Wed–Mon • Adm charge

9 Château de Creully
In the same family since 1613, this château has retained its original Louis XIII decoration. It was from this castle that the BBC reported on the D-Day landings. ◈ Map D3 • 02 31 80 18 65 • Open Jul–Sep: Wed–Mon.

10 Château de Pontécoulant
Fronted by long, formal lawns, backed by woodland, this 16th–18th-century château in the Suisse Normande has great charm. ◈ Map D4 • 02 31 69 62 54 • Open mid-Mar–mid-Oct: Tue–Sun • Adm charge

For more Norman châteaux **See pp81, 100**

Left **Memorial gardens, Abbaye d'Ardenne, Caen** Right **Abbaye Notre-Dame, Le Bec-Hellouin**

🔟 Religious Buildings

1 Abbaye d'Ardennes, Caen
During the Battle of Normandy, 23 Canadian soldiers were executed at this 12th-century abbey on the outskirts of Caen; a memorial garden now commemorates them. The partially ruined abbey church is a fine example of Norman Gothic architecture. ◈ Map D3

2 Abbaye St-Martin-de-Mondaye, Juaye-Mondaye
The monks of this small community welcome guests on retreat, and host summer concerts in their handsome 18th-century abbey. ◈ Map D3

3 Prieuré de St-Gabriel, Brécy
Set around a courtyard, the lovely honey-stone buildings of this former daughter house of the Abbey of Fécamp are now occupied by a horticultural school. They can be viewed from the outside only. ◈ Map D3

4 St-Pierre, Thaon
No longer in use, this little church is a lovely sight in its isolated setting, hidden by greenery at the tip of a valley. A gem of Romanesque architecture. ◈ Map D3

5 Eglise Abbatiale, St-Pierre-sur-Dives
At noon, the copper strip on the floor of the nave shows the position of the sun's rays (see p33). ◈ Map E4

6 Ste-Foy, Conches-en-Ouche
This Flamboyant Gothic church is graced by some of the finest stained glass in Normandy (see p90). Its tall spire is a precise copy of the one knocked down in a storm in 1842. ◈ Map H4

7 Abbaye Notre-Dame, Le Bec-Hellouin
There is a marvellous view of the abbey, its creamy 18th-century buildings nestling in the lush valley, as you enter the village from the south on the D39. The 18th-century refectory has been converted into a simple church, where its founder's sarcophagus lies sunk beneath the altar (see p46). ◈ Map H3

8 Notre-Dame, Louviers
From the 13th century, the town was an important centre of cloth-making. The lavishly deco-rated church, with its stunning south porch, reflects its wealth. ◈ Map J3

9 Notre-Dame, Verneuil-sur-Avre
Built of a reddish stone called grison, this attractive church is noted for its plethora of saintly statues, mostly 16th-century (see p90). ◈ Map H5

10 Notre-Dame, Vernon
With its elegant High Gothic west front, complete with graceful rose window, this collegiate church has the feel of a cathedral. ◈ Map K4

For more Norman abbeys See pp46–7

Left **Horse-racing at Deauville** Right **Canoeing on the Risle**

🔟 Recreational Activities

1 Les Virevoltés, Vire
Don't miss this wacky annual street festival, with acrobats, dancers and much more. ⬡ *Map C5 • 1st 2 weeks July • Tourist office: sq de la Résistance. 02 31 66 28 50*

2 Horse-racing, Deauville
Free guided tours are held on race days at Deauville's two immaculate racecourses. ⬡ *Map E3 • Tourist office: 112 rue Victor Hugo. 02 31 14 40 00*

3 Casinos, La Côte Fleurie
There are casinos (for adults only) at Cabourg, Houlgate, Villers-sur-Mer, Deauville and Trouville – the latter two being wonderfully florid turn-of-the-century edifices *(see pp26–7)*. ⬡ *Map E3*

4 Espace Nautile, Lisieux
In bad weather, an indoor swimming pool can be a godsend; the best is here, with a 54 m (180 ft) slide. ⬡ *25 rue Guillonneau • Map F4 • 02 31 48 66 66*

5 Canoeing on the Risle
Hire a canoe or kayak for a lazy descent of the lovely River Risle. ⬡ *Les Castors Rislois, Pont-Audemer: Map G3. 02 32 56 04 15 • Base de Loisirs: 6 blvd de la République, Brionne. Map H3. 02 32 45 44 40*

6 Canoeing on the Eure
Another delightful canoe or kayak trip, on the beautiful stretch of the Eure north of Pacy *(see p89)*. ⬡ *rue du Manoir, Autheuil-Authouillet • Map J4 • 02 32 35 16 46*

7 Eur'Autruche, Beaumesnil
If you crave close contact with ostriches, Eur'Autruche is the place to go, especially in mid-May, when the babies are hatched. As well as meeting the ostriches, you can buy feathers, eggs and ostrich steaks. ⬡ *rte du Château d'Eau • Map H4 • 02 32 44 40 41 • Open 3–6pm weekends & public hols; Jul–Aug: daily*

8 Bike-rail Rides
The *vélo-rail* "bike" is a four-seater buggy that runs on disused railway lines in La Suisse Normande *(see p88)*. Two of the seats have pedals to power the bike. ⬡ *from Pont Erambourg & Pont du Coudray/Val de Maizet • Map D5 • 02 31 69 39 30 • www.rails-suissenormande.fr*

9 Boat Trips and Canal Cruises, Caen
Two separate trips can be taken depending on the day of the week. Either cruise the beautiful Caen Canal from Bassin St-Pierre, or sail from Pegasus Bridge *(see p29)* to the D-Day beaches and La Côte Fleurie. ⬡ *Map D3 • Les Vedettes de Normandie: 02 31 43 86 12*

10 Souterroscope, Caumont-l'Eventé
With 125 m (410 ft) of tunnels, strange rocks, beautiful minerals and even an underground rainbow, this former slate mine is a good choice for a rainy day. ⬡ *rte de St-Lô • Map C4 • 02 31 71 15 15 • Open Jun–Aug: daily; Sep–mid-Dec, Feb–May: Tue–Sun • Adm charge*

Left **Après La Pluie, Beaumont-en-Auge** Right **Umbrellas at H20 Parapluies, Creully**

Local Specialities

1 Gribouille, Honfleur
For more than 20 years, jovial M Gribouille has sold the best of Norman gastronomic specialities, from *pommeau* to *confiture du lait (see p57)*, in his lavish emporium in Vieux Honfleur.
◈ *rue de l'Homme de Bois • Map F3*

2 A La Recherche du Temps Perdu, Cabourg
Ghislaine and Sylvie Soulas sell clothes, knitwear, embroidery, linens, gifts and traditional games in this enchanting boutique.
◈ *3 ave Commdt Touchard • Map E3*

3 Poterie du Mesnil de Bavent, Ranville
Famous for its roof decorations and finials (*épis de faitage*), this pottery also produces faïence animals, many of them life-size, as well as hand-decorated table-ware. ◈ *Le Mesnil, D513 • Map E3*

4 Après La Pluie, Beaumont-en-Auge
Kaleidoscopes galore, plus thaumascopes, phenakistiscopes, fantascopes, praxinoscopes and other absorbing optical objects from a manufacturer unique in Europe. ◈ *3 rue de la Libération • Map E3*

5 H20 Parapluies, Creully
The creation of handcrafted umbrellas is an art, and it is practised to perfection at H20. From plain about-town umbrellas to unique creations, the factory shop has a wide selection.
◈ *Hameau de Creullet • Map D3*

6 Calvados Dupont, Victot-Pontfol
One of the most impressive of the 20 or so producers along the Route du Cidre *(see p33)*. As well as cider, Calvados and *pommeau*, you can buy Crème Calvados, cider vinegar and Pomme Captive – with the apple a "prisoner" in the bottle. ◈ *RD16 • Map E4*

7 Calvados Pierre Huet, Cambremer
Another traditional producer in the heart of cider country, Huet has operated from the lovely half-timbered Manoir de la Brière des Fontaines since 1865. You can visit the atmospheric cider distillery before buying. ◈ *Map E4*

8 Le Village Fromager, Livarot
Cheese is hugely important in Central Normandy. At this centre you can watch cheeses being made, before tasting samples such as Pont l'Evêque and Neufchâtel *(see p69)*.

9 La Ferme du Mesnil, Ste-Marguerite-en-Ouche
Foie gras, *rillettes* and *confits* from a farm deep in the Pays d'Ouche. ◈ *Map H4*

10 Miel Charozé, La Vacquerie
The art of beekeeping is explained at this lovely, isolated farm, whose shop sells wonderful honey and a huge variety of honey-based products. ◈ *Map C4 • Le Haut Hamel*

Price Categories

For a three course meal for one with half a bottle of wine (or equivalent meal), taxes and extra charges.

€	under €30
€€	€30–€40
€€€	€40–€50
€€€€	€50–€60
€€€€€	over €60

Belle Île-sur-Risle, Pont-Audemer

🔟 Places to Eat

1 Le Pressoir, Caen
Ivan Vautier has a Michelin star for his innovative take on Norman cooking: *pigeonneau* and *tartare de langoustine*, for example. ⊗ *3 ave Henry Cheron • Map D3 • 02 31 73 32 71 • Closed Sun D, Mon • €€€€*

2 Auberge le Clos Saint Julien, St Julien sur Calonne
A charming country inn run by a talented Alsatian chef who blends the flavours of Alsace with local cheeses and pork. ⊗ *Map E3 • 02 31 64 08 64 • Closed Tue D, Wed, Sun D • €€*

3 Auberge des Deux Tonneaux, Pierrefitte-en-Auge
This 17th-century inn offers gorgeous views and traditional country fare such as suckling pig. ⊗ *Le Bourg • Map G3 • 02 31 64 09 31 • Closed Tue (exc Jul & Aug) • No dis. access • €€*

4 Au P'tit Normand, Cambremer-en-Auge
This snug bistro is a local favourite for home-made terrines, mixed salads and Norman classics. ⊗ *pl de l'Église • Map E4 • 02 31 32 03 20 • Closed Sun D, Mon, Jan–mid-Feb • €*

5 Les Vapeurs, Trouville
Fabulous *moules* with *frites*, desserts with lashings of *crème fraîche* and crisp white wines ensure this place is always bustling. ⊗ *160–162 quai Fernand Moureaux • Map E3 • 02 31 88 15 24 • €€€*

6 Belle Île-sur-Risle, Pont-Audemer
A romantic private island provides the setting for Mme Yazbeck's elegant mansion hotel and restaurant. The *pastilla de lapin* (in filo) is wonderful. ⊗ *112 rte de Rouen • Map G3 • 02 32 56 96 22 • Closed mid-Nov–mid-Mar • €€€*

7 Le Bréard, Honfleur
At this elegant restaurant, chef Fabrice Sébire prepares stylish dishes from local ingredients. ⊗ *7 rue du Puits • Map F3 • 02 31 89 53 40 • Closed Wed L, Mon, Tue (exc Jul & Sep: open daily, D only) • €€€€*

8 Le Bistrot d'à Côté, Port-en-Bessin
The blue-and-white decor fits the harbourside setting of this bistro. The seafood is deliciously fresh. ⊗ *12 rue Michel Lefournier • Map C3 • 02 31 51 79 12 • Closed Sun–Mon (except Jul–Aug: closed Mon) • €€*

9 La Ferme de la Haute Crémonville, St-Étienne-du-Vauvray
Beautiful, half-timbered Norman farm serving tasty, local dishes. The meat is cooked on an open fire. ⊗ *rte de Crémonville • Map J3 • 02 32 59 14 22 • Closed Wed D, Sat L, Sun • €€–€€€*

10 La Fine Fourchette, Falaise
Just outside town, a glowing dining room and Norman dishes with a twist of sophistication. ⊗ *52 rue Georges Clemenceau • Map E4 • 02 31 90 08 59 • Closed Tue D in winter • €€*

Unless otherwise stated, all restaurants accept credit cards and serve vegetarian meals.

Left **Harbour and upper town, Granville** Right **Omonville-la-Petite, Hague Peninsula**

Northwestern Normandy

NORMANDY'S NORTHWEST IS A WORLD OF ITS OWN. *Thrusting into the English Channel is the Cotentin Peninsula, with picturesque little ports, long, unspoilt beaches, and gannets and shearwaters wheeling in the sky above wild and windblown headlands. Cotentin's proud maritime heritage is evident, especially in the important strategic port and naval base of Cherbourg, and it was from here in the Middle Ages that the descendants of Norse settlers set sail to establish kingdoms in Sicily and southern Italy.*

Further south, in the heart of the region – which encompasses the département of Manche – lies the marshy landscape of the Marais du Cotentin et du Bessin, a paradise for nature lovers. Further south, there are meadows and hedgerows (bocage), and the lovely River Vire, seemingly made for pleasure.

Coutances Cathedral with its lantern tower

Sights

1. Utah Beach
2. Cherbourg
3. La Hague Peninsula
4. Parc Régional des Marais du Cotentin
5. Lessay
6. Coutances
7. Vallée de la Vire
8. Abbaye de Hambye
9. Granville
10. Villedieu-les-Poêles

1 Utah Beach

On D-Day, 6 June 1944, the eastern coast of the Cotentin Peninsula, code-named Utah Beach, received thousands of American troops, backed up by paratroops dropped inland around Ste-Mère-Eglise *(see pp28–31)*. 🅼 *Map B3*

2 Cherbourg

There's more than meets the eye to Cherbourg, and of particular note is La Cité de la Mer, which is Europe's deepest aquarium *(see p52)*. For a good view of the port, drive to the hill-top Fort du Roule, which houses the Musée de la Libération, recalling the events leading to Cherbourg's liberation on 27 June 1944. Most activity is centred on the flower-filled market square, pl Général-de-Gaulle, and along shopping streets such as rue Tour-Carrée and rue de la Paix. The town's collection of fine art in the spacious Musée Thomas-Henry includes portraits by Jean-François Millet *(see p101)*. Parc Emmanuel Liais has small botanical gardens and a densely packed Musée d'Histoire Naturelle. 🅼 *Map B2 • Tourist office: 2 quai Alexandre III. 02 33 93 52 02*

3 La Hague Peninsula

Calm and lovely on a sunny spring day, rugged and wind-swept during a winter storm, this furthest prong of Cotentin is stunningly beautiful. Its stone villages, majestic cliffs, jagged rocks and hidden coves are more reminiscent of Brittany than Normandy, and the presence of a vast nuclear power station slap in the middle does not detract – at least too much – from the glorious coastline *(see p101)*. 🅼 *Map A2 • Tourist office: 45 rue Jallot, Beaumont-Hague. 02 33 52 74 94*

4 Parc Régional des Marais du Cotentin

The band of low-lying marshes and water meadows stretching across the base of the Cotentin Peninsula has been formed into a fascinating regional park with a rich birdlife, as well as houses made of clay and straw. Carentan is the gateway town, with a reception centre at Les Ponts d'Ouve (on the D913 between Carentan and St-Côme-du-Mont), in the centre of a watery land-scape. An exhibition and video introduce the park to visitors, who explore on foot or by boat. 🅼 *Map B3 • Espace de Découverte: Les Ponts d'Ouve, St-Côme-du-Mont. 02 33 71 65 30*

5 Lessay

The compact and comforting lines of Lessay's abbey church, St-Trinité, make it one of the most beautiful Romanesque buildings in Normandy. Dating from 1098, it was almost destroyed in 1944, but has been magnificently reconstructed using original materials. The interior is plain and lovely, with fine stained glass adding warmth. Sleepy Lessay's big moment comes in the second week of September, when thousands converge for the convivial three-day Foire de Ste-Croix *(see p73)*. 🅼 *Map B3 • Tourist office: 11 pl St-Cloud. 02 33 45 14 34*

Church of St Trinité, Lessay

Vallée de la Vire

6 Coutances

One somehow doesn't expect to find a great cathedral in this isolated corner of France, but here it is: a soaring stone rocket crowning the hill around which the town is gathered. In the 13th century, with the aid of the de Hauteville family, who had prospered in Sicily and southern Italy, a new Norman Gothic building was surmounted on the remains of the previous, fire-damaged Romanesque one. Its remarkable octagonal lantern above the altar rises to 41 m (135 ft), and its many towers, spires and pointed arches sweep the eye skyward. In town, the flower-filled Jardin des Plantes makes a perfect setting for some of the concerts that take place in Coutances during the annual Jazz sous les Pommiers festival in May *(see p72)*. ◈ *Map B4 • Tourist office: pl Georges Leclerc. 02 33 19 08 10*

Le Bocage

A rolling landscape of mixed woodland and meadow, bordered by banks topped with high, thick hedgerows, bisected by narrow, sunken lanes – this is the *bocage* that covers much of Normandy, particularly around St-Lô and Vire. Pastoral in peacetime, it proved a nightmare for the Allies in 1944, making progress against the enemy near impossible.

7 Vallée de la Vire

As it winds towards the sea, the River Vire cuts deeply through granite schists to form a ribbon of water amid glorious countryside. Towpaths border most of the river between Vire and St-Lô, so you can picnic, cycle, walk or horse-ride alongside. Condé-sur-Vire is the place for canoeing, while at Roches de Ham, the granite terrain leaps up to form a towering 80 m (260 ft) rock face above the river. Here are magnificent views of the verdant valley – and a welcome little crêperie and cider bar in summer. Nearby, La Chapelle-sur-Vire makes a perfect picnic spot. The grandiose chapel that dominates the village has been a place of pilgrimage since the 12th century. At Torigni-sur-Vire, the Château de Matignon houses a fine collection of tapestries. ◈ *Map C4 • Tourist office: pl Général-de-Gaulle, St-Lô. 02 33 77 60 35*

8 Abbaye de Hambye

Tucked beneath a wooded escarpment by the River Sienne, Hambye's roofless remains have an immediately calming effect on visitors. The monastic buildings of this 12th-century Benedictine abbey have been restored and host exhibitions and concerts. ◈ *Map B4 • Open Apr–Oct: 10am–noon, 2–6pm Wed–Mon • Adm charge*

9 Granville

At first sight, Granville seems an unlikely setting for one of Normandy's most popular seaside resorts *(see p61)*, but it has two distinct faces. Ramparts enclose the upper town, which sits on a rocky spur overlooking the Baie du Mont-St-Michel. The walled town developed from fortifications built by the English in 1439 as part of their assault on the Mont. The Musée de Vieux Granville, in the town gatehouse, recounts Granville's long-established seafaring tradition. The chapel walls of the Église de Notre-Dame are lined with tributes from local fishermen to their patroness, Notre Dame du Cap Lihou. The lower town is the resort, with casino, promenades and public gardens. From the port, there are boat trips to the Îles Chausey, a scattering of low-lying granite islands. ✪ Map B5 • Tourist office: 4 cours Jonville. 02 33 91 30 03

Villedieu-les-Poêles

Since the 13th-century, this pretty little town – in every nook and cranny of which there are copper pots and pans for sale – has been the capital of copper (see p65). In the Atelier de Cuivre, you can see craftsmen at work, while the atmospheric Fonderie des Cloches gives a fascinating insight into the making of bells (clay, horse dung and goat hair are some unlikely components). Another local craft, lace-making, is explained at the Musée de la Poeslerie. ✪ Map B5 • Tourist office: 8 pl des Costils. 02 33 61 05 69

Copper workshop, Villedieu-les-Poêles

A Day in Cotentin

Morning

Leave Cherbourg on the D901 toward St-Pierre-Église. After 15 km (9 miles), turn onto the D355 to pretty **Le Vast** in the heart of the lovely **Val de Saire**. Be sure to buy a delicious brioche du Vast from Olivier Thebault, 12 les Moulins. Follow the river on the D25 to Valcanville, then on the D125 to **La Pernelle**, climbing the steep granite hill to the church and, above, a magnificent panorama of the coast.

In **St-Vaast-la-Hougue** (see p100), book a table for lunch (don't forget to try some St-Vaast oysters) at **France et des Fuchsias** (see p103), then stock up on food and wine at the family-run emporium **Gosselin**, trading since 1889. If there's time, take a trip to **Île de Tatihou**, just offshore (see p102).

Afternoon

From St-Vaast, it's a quick drive along the D14 to Quineville, then the coastal D421 to **Utah Beach** to contemplate the events of June 1944 (see pp28–31). After a bracing walk along the beach and dunes, head inland to **Ste-Mère-Église** (see p100) and its famous church (see p28), perhaps pausing for refreshment at Café de la Libération in rue Général-de-Gaulle.

From Ste-Mère-Église, drive into the watery heart of the Cotentin marshlands (see p97), ending the day on the banks of the Douve at Les Moitiers-en-Bauptois at the delightful **Auberge de l'Ouve** (open Apr–Oct; 02 33 21 16 26), where local eels are the speciality.

Left **St-Lô** Right **Château de Pirou**

TOP 10 Best of the Rest

1 St-Vaast-la-Hougue and Île de Tatihou
The harbour of this enchanting small port was fortified after the French naval defeat in 1692, as was the Île de Tatihou – now the site of a garden, bird-watching post and maritime museum. ⊗ Map B2 • Tourist office: 1 pl Général-de-Gaulle. 02 33 23 19 32

2 Valognes
Though badly damaged in 1944, Valognes retains traces of its glory days as the "Versailles of the North", including the splendid Hôtel de Beaumont. ⊗ Map B2 • Tourist office: pl du Château. 02 33 40 11 55

3 Bricquebec
This quiet town is noted for its Trappist monastery and its old castle. ⊗ Map B2 • Tourist office: 13 pl Ste-Anne. 02 33 52 21 65

4 Barneville-Carteret
This lively resort is formed by the villages of Barneville, Carteret and Barneville-Plage (see p61). Its rocky headland, Cap de Carteret, makes a bracing walk. ⊗ Map A3 • Tourist office: 10 rue des Écoles. 02 33 04 90 58

5 St-Sauveur-le-Vicomte
The 12th-century castle houses the Musée Barbey-d'Aurevilly, dedicated to the 19th-century novelist who was born in the town (see p50). ⊗ Map B3 • 02 33 21 50 44 • Open Oct–May: Tue, Thu & Fri; Jun & Sep: Tue–Sat; Jul–Aug: Mon–Sat & Sun pm • Adm charge

6 Ste-Mère-Église
Apart from its war museum and church, made famous by the film The Longest Day, the town is known for its livestock market. Rural life in the early 1900s is illustrated at the Ferme Musée du Cotentin. ⊗ Map B3 • Tourist office: rue Eisenhower. 02 33 21 00 33

7 Abbaye de Cérisy-la-Fôret
This Benedictine abbey was founded in 1032 by Duke Robert the Magnificent. Much of the nave is now missing, but it still serves as a reminder of the former importance of monasteries. ⊗ Map C3 • Open Easter–Nov: daily • Adm charge

8 St-Lô
The strongest draw in the regional capital, which was unsympathetically rebuilt after wartime destruction, is the Haras (national stud), where you can inspect 100 stallions of different breeds. ⊗ Map C4 • Tourist office: pl Général-de-Gaulle. 02 33 77 60 35

9 Château de Pirou
Set on an island in the middle of an artificial lake, this remote 12th-century fortress is a stirring sight. ⊗ Map B4 • Open mid-Mar–Sep, mid-Oct–mid-Nov: Wed–Mon • Adm charge

10 Château de Gratot
The roofless remains of this once-great château, the ancestral home of the Argouges family, lie in quiet countryside. An exhibition tells its story. ⊗ Map B4 • 02 33 45 18 49 • Open daily • Adm charge

Left **Gruchy** Right **Omonville-la-Petite**

TOP 10 Highlights of the Cotentin Coast

1 Val de Saire
The gentle prettiness of this verdant valley east of Barfleur is in sharp contrast to the wild coastline *(see p99)*. ◈ *Map B2*

2 Barfleur
It is said that William the Conqueror's invasion vessel was built in this delightful fishing port *(see p62)*. Its lighthouse, at Gatteville, is one of the tallest in France, with 365 steps to the top; when you get there, the reward is a fine panorama. ◈ *Map B2*

3 Querqueville
Beside the hilltop church, surrounded by a cemetery packed with ornate marble tombs, stands St-Germain, the oldest (10th century) chapel in western France. ◈ *Map A2*

4 Château de Nacqueville
The park of this 16th-century château, with its romantic turreted gatehouse, is loveliest in May and June when the rhododendrons are in bloom. ◈ *Map A2*
• Open May–Sep: noon–5pm Tue, Thu, Fri, Sun & public hols • Adm charge

5 Gruchy
This spruce seaside village includes the humble birthplace of Jean-François Millet *(see p48)*, open to the public in summer. Walk to the dramatic Rocher du Castel-Vendon; Millet's depiction of it can be seen in the Musée Thomas-Henry in Cherbourg *(see p97)*. ◈ *Map A2*

6 Omonville-la-Petite
The pretty churchyard here contains the natural, uncarved headstone of poet Jacques Prévert, as well as those of his wife and daughter. Nearby is his house, open to the public in summer *(see p51)*. ◈ *Map A2*

7 Port Racine
En route to Cap de la Hague, France's smallest port is tucked beneath the road. From here, follow signs to Jardins Prévert, an oasis at the head of a wild valley. ◈ *Map A2*

8 St-Germain-des-Vaux
This tiny, tranquil village offers the perfect lunch stop – at Le Moulin à Vent *(see p103)*.

9 Nez de Jobourg
The desolate Baie d'Ecalgrain sweeps round to this impressive promontory. From here, the road to Vauville is dominated by the huge Usine Atomique de la Hague nuclear power station. ◈ *Map A2*

10 Vauville
The subtropical gardens of Château de Vauville and a beach perfect for sand yachting are the twin attractions here. ◈ *Map A2*

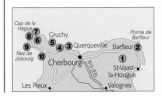

Left **Amphibious craft to the Île de Tatihou** Right **Musée Christian Dior**

🔟 Family Outings

1 La Cité de la Mer, Cherbourg
Man's conquest of the deep is the theme of Cherbourg's former Gare Maritime Transatlantique, an Art Deco jewel. Experience what it's like to live aboard a nuclear submarine (no children under six) *(see p52)*.

2 L'Attelage des Grandes Marées, Gouville-sur-Mer
Here you can visit an oyster park at low tide by horse-drawn carriage. ✪ *Map B4 • 02 33 47 86 13 or 06 88 78 36 75 (booking essential)*

3 Manoir de Dur-Ecu
This lovely ancestral manor house hides a delightful surprise for children: a maize maze, designed by English maze-maker Adrian Fisher. ✪ *Map A2 • Open Jul–Sep: 11am–1pm, 3–7pm Tue–Thu*

4 Mini-trains
Two mini-trains operate in the region: one along the coast from Carteret to Portbail, the other through marshland from St-Lô to Periers. ✪ *Train du Cotentin: Map A3. 02 33 04 70 08 • Mini-train des Marais: C3–B3. 02 33 07 91 77*

5 Watersports
The *Jolie France* sails from Granville to Chausey's Grand-Île. Cherbourg offers a range of watersports, from rowing and kayaking to sedate pleasure cruises. ✪ *Jolie France: 02 33 50 31 81. www.vedettejoliefrance • Cherbourg: www.cherbourg-hague-nautisme.com*

6 Île de Tatihou
Children enjoy the amphibious craft that takes them across to this tiny pleasure island with a fascinating history, just off St-Vaast-la-Hougue *(see p100)*.

7 Boating round St-Lô
As a reminder of the ferocity of war, St-Lô's Notre-Dame church has been left virtually untouched after its bombardment *(see p100)*; the ramparts also remain, and you can see these sights while gliding by on a barge on the River Vire. ✪ *from quai à Tangue Plage Verte • Map C4 • 02 33 05 33 81*

8 Ferme aux 5 Saisons, Flamanville
A farm for children: see an apple press in action; visit the animals; bake bread for tea. ✪ *Map A2 • 02 33 04 56 84 • Open Jul & Aug: pm Mon–Fri*

9 Musée Christian Dior
Mothers and daughters in particular will be drawn to the exhibition of designs by Dior and other top couturiers in Dior's childhood house, set in a lovely clifftop garden. ✪ *Map B5 • Les Rhumbs, Granville. 02 33 61 48 21 • Open mid-May–end Sep: daily • Adm charge*

10 Vélorail, Vallée de la Vire
Ride the (disused) railways in a pedal-powered buggy. ✪ *Condé-sur-Vire • Map C4 • 02 33 05 46 55 • www.velorail-pourlavire.fr • Open Jul & Aug: daily (exc Mon am); mid-Apr–Jun & Sep: weekends, public hols*

Price Categories

For a three course meal for one with half a bottle of wine (or equivalent meal), taxes and extra charges.

€ under €30
€€ €30–€40
€€€ €40–€50
€€€€ €50–€60
€€€€€ over €60

Le Moulin à Vent, St-Germain-des-Vaux

TOP 10 Places to Eat

1 Au Bouquet de Cosqueville, Cosqueville

This charming hotel-restaurant on a sheltered cove east of Cherbourg offers fine seafood dishes and delicious Normandy cheeses. Ⓢ Hameau Remond • Map B2 • 02 33 54 32 81 • Closed Mon (Oct–Apr) • €€€

2 Le Moulin à Vent, St-Germain-des-Vaux

Glorious views and the freshest seafood at very reasonable prices (see p101). Ⓢ Hameau Danneville • Map A3 • 02 33 52 75 20 • Closed Wed & Thu except Jul–Aug • €€

3 France et des Fuchsias, St-Vaast-la-Hougue

If you like seafood, you'll love France et des Fuchsias (see p126). Ⓢ 20 rue Maréchal Foch • Map B2 • 02 33 54 40 41 • Closed Mon, Tue L • €€

4 Hôtel Moderne, Barfleur

Run by chef Frédéric Cauchemez, this charming restaurant is near Barfleur's placid harbour. Menus run from bargain lunches to gourmet feasts, with original creations based on the catch-of-the-day fish. Ⓢ pl du Général de Gaulle • Map B2 • 02 33 23 12 44 • Closed Tue D, Wed, Mon Jul–Aug, Mon–Tue Nov–Mar • €€€

5 La Ferme des Mares, Saint-Germain-sur-Ay

This restaurant, once a fortified Norman farm, serves the best local fish, lamb and traditional cheeses. Ⓢ Map B3 • 02 33 17 01 02 • Closed Wed, Sun D • €€€

6 Auberge de Goury, Auderville

At the very end of Cap de la Hague, this restaurant serves fruits de mer, and fresh fish and meats grilled over an open fire. Ⓢ porte de Goury • Map A2 • 02 33 52 77 01 • Closed Sun D, Mon • €€€

7 La Plancha, Agon-Coutainville

This trendy beach brasserie has fabulous sea views and an original menu of seafood and fish platters and tapas. Ⓢ 77 rue Dramard • Map B2 • 02 33 47 26 77 • Closed Tue & Wed (Sep–Jun) • €€

8 Verte Campagne, Trelly

Elegantly rustic on the inside, this old, ivy-covered farmhouse offers well-prepared dishes spread over a wide enough range of menus to suit most pockets (see p128). Ⓢ Map B4 • 02 33 47 65 33 • Closed Wed • €€€

9 Ferme de Malte, Villedieu-les-Poêles

Owned by the Knights of Malta, who have a long connection with the town, this smart restaurant specializes in fish and has two dining rooms. Ⓢ 11 rue Tétrel • Map B5 • 02 33 91 35 91 • Closed Wed D, Sun D, Mon • €€€

10 L'Auberge, Mesnil-Rogues

Hams and legs of lamb are spit-roasted by chef Yves Toquet at this rustic auberge. The fish is good too. Ⓢ Map B4 • 02 33 61 37 12 • Closed Tue D, Wed D, Sun D, Mon • €

Following pages **Produce at Caen market**

Left **Château de Carrouges** Right **Établissement Thermal, Bagnoles de l'Orne**

Southern Normandy

ROM THE ASTONISHING SIGHT OF MONT-ST-MICHEL, *appearing like
some fabulous mirage out of the pancake-flat landscape which surrounds
it, to the equine elegance of the national stud at Haras du Pin or the human
elegance of romantic Château d'O, this region, which consists of the
département of Orne and the southern part of Manche, is crammed with
history and variety. The scenery is just as varied: there's the rugged beauty
of the Pays d'Alençon in the Parc Régional de Normandie-Maine, where
bands of thick forest cover the high ridges; the wooded Mortainais, with its
steep valleys and exhilarating waterfalls; the gently rolling pastureland of
the Perche, interrupted by cool, deep, green forests; the narrow lanes and
pretty, flower-filled villages of the Pays du Bocage Ornais; and those flat salt
marshes of the Baie de Mont-St-Michel.*

🔟 Sights

1. Mont-St-Michel
2. Avranches
3. Alençon
4. Bagnoles de l'Orne
5. Le Perche
6. Haras National du Pin
7. Parc Naturel Régional de Normandie-Maine
8. Château d'O
9. Château de Carrouges
10. Alpes Mancelles

Mont-St-Michel with local sheep

Mont-St-Michel

Despite being the most photographed sight in France, the ethereal beauty of this vast abbey can still take your breath away *(see pp8–11)*.

Avranches

Avranches has a long and historic association with Mont-St-Michel *(see pp8–11)*, which it overlooks across the bay (one of the best views is from the Jardin des Plantes). St Aubert, who founded the abbey there, was Bishop of Avranches; his skull, complete with the hole made by St Michael's finger, is on display in the Basilique de St-Gervais et St-Protais. In an annexe of the former episcopal palace, the Musée d'Avranches contains wonderful collections of medieval sculpture and religious art, and in the town hall library you can see the superb Mont-St-Michel manuscripts, dating back to the 8th century. ✆ *Map B5 • Tourist office: 2 rue du Général de Gaulle. 02 33 58 00 22*

Alençon

This handsome market town was a famous lacemaking centre in the 17th and 18th centuries. The only examples you will see today are displayed in the Musée de la Dentelle "au Point d'Alençon", housed in General Leclerc's wartime headquarters, and in the Musée des Beaux-Arts et de la Dentelle. The latter presents an exhaustive history of the lace industry, along with collections of French paintings and Cambodian artifacts. Even the intricate stonework on the façade of the Église de Notre-Dame resembles lace. Inside, a chapel is dedicated to Ste Thérèse, born in the town and baptized here. ✆ *Map E6 • Tourist office: Maison d'Ozé, pl de la Magdelaine. 02 33 80 66 33*

Jardins des Plantes, Avranches

Bagnoles-de-l'Orne

Clamber to the top of the Roc au Chien for a panorama of this refined spa town steeped in legend *(see p61)*, its lake, casino, park and avenues of gracious houses built for the wealthy who came to take the waters in the late 19th century. Sufferers from problems ranging from arthritis to stress still flock to the Établissement Thermal in its striking *belle époque* building. ✆ *Map D5 • Tourist office: pl du Marché. 02 33 37 85 66*

Le Perche

Still relatively unknown, this area is famous for its powerful Percheron horses and its manors. Perche manors are quite different from typical cosy, half-timbered Norman farmhouses; they are much more defensive buildings of stone, embellished with turrets and towers. The surrounding countryside is gentle, with undulating hills, dense forest and lush valleys. Grazing Percherons add an air of serenity. Chief among its seductive villages and small towns are Mortagne and Bellême *(see p110)*. ✆ *Map G6, G7 • Comité Départementale du Tourisme: 88 rue St-Blaise, Alençon. 02 33 28 88 71*

For more on lacemaking **See p64**

Haras National du Pin

6 Haras National du Pin

You don't have to be a horse lover to be impressed by the style and splendour of the national stud, a "Versailles for horses" founded by Colbert in the mid-17th century with the approval of the Sun King himself. Colbert commissioned Pierre Le Mousseux, a protégé of Mansart, to design it. At the end of a long, grassy ride carved through the surrounding woods, the main château and two elegant stable blocks (now housing exhibits) enclose a horseshoe-shaped courtyard known as Colbert's Court, the scene of horse and carriage displays on Thursday afternoons in summer. There are guided tours of the forge, tack room and stables, where some 100 stallions are kept at stud.

Ⓢ Le Pin-au-Haras • Map E5 • 02 33 36 68 68 • www.haras-national-du-pin.com • Open Apr–Sep: 10am–6pm daily; Mar & Oct: Sat & Sun. Tours every half hour • Adm charge

Horses

In stud farms throughout Orne, Manche and Calvados, horses of the highest calibre are bred, raised and trained for competition. The four main breeds are: thoroughbreds – spirited, highly-strung racehorses; Norman trotters, a mixed breed with a longer track career; cobs – sturdy carriage horses; and Percherons, ideal for heavy farm work.

7 Parc Naturel Régional de Normandie-Maine

With a landscape marked by escarpments and forests in the haut pays of the Alpes Mancelles, and by rolling hills, bocage and open country in the bas pays at Saosnois and around Alençon and Sées, this vast natural park dips south from Basse-Normandie into the départements of Mayenne and Sarthe in the Pays-de-Loire. Start at the Maison du Parc in Carrouges, where you'll find maps and itineraries. There is also an information centre at the Comptoir du Parc in Alençon, and nature centres are scattered throughout the park (see p42). Ⓢ Map D5, E5 • Maison du Parc: Carrouges. 02 33 81 13 33 • Open Jan–Apr, Oct–Dec: Tue–Fri; May–Sep: Tue–Sun

8 Château d'O

Fairy-tale turrets, carved pediments and steep-sloping roofs reflected in the limpid, green waters of its rectangular moat: this early-Renaissance château is as enchanting as the family name is curious. It was built mainly during the 15th and 16th centuries, with a west wing – now the living quarters – added in the 18th. You can wander in the grounds or take a short tour of the interior, furnished in predominantly 18th-century style.

Ⓢ Mortrée • Map E5 • Opening times vary: phone Orne tourist office for details. 02 33 28 88 71 (1 Aug–9 Sep: 02 33 39 55 79) • Free

Château de Carrouges

9 Until 1936, when it was bought by the state, this imposing red-brick château had been in the Le Veneur de Tillières family for almost 500 years. Founded by Jean de Carrouges in the 14th century, it has all the attributes of a grand château: moats, terraces, a park and gardens, and a particularly elegant 16th-century gatehouse with four pepperpot towers *(see p112)*. ◈ *Map E6* • *02 33 27 20 32* • *Open Apr–Jun & Sep: 10am–noon, 2–6pm; Mar & Oct: 10am–noon, 2–5pm*

Alpes Mancelles

10 In the Parc Naturel Régional de Normandie-Maine on the southern border of Normandy is this landscape of plunging hills, steep valleys and forests. Not quite comparable with the Alps, it is more rugged (particularly around the Sarthe Valley) than the rest of the region. At 417 m (1,368 ft), Mont des Avaloirs, to the west of Alençon, is joint highest point in western France. Among its charming villages, St-Céneri-le-Gérei is the jewel *(see p110)*. ◈ *Map E6* • *Tourist office: 19 ave du Docteur Riant, Fresnay-sur-Sarthe. 02 43 33 28 04. Closed Mon*

Alpes Mancelles

Exploring the Perche

Morning

Pick up a "Circuit du Patrimoine" from the tourist office in the old market in **Mortagne-au-Perche** (pl du Général-de-Gaulle), and walk its route, popping into the Église de Notre-Dame to see the glorious altarpiece *(see p110)*. Finish with a coffee in the **Hôtel Tribunal** *(see p113)*.

Leave Mortagne-au-Perche on the D931 toward Mamers. Turn left on the D275 and follow signs to **La Perrière**, an enchanting village of colourful cottages and tempting *brocantes* (antiques shops), with a glorious view. Take the RF225 through the peaceful **Forêt de Bellême** *(see p67)* as far as the D931. Turn right for **Bellême** *(see p110)*. Go through the town and turn right onto the D203 to Nocé, where the **Auberge des 3J** (1 pl Docteur-Gireaux) is an excellent lunch stop.

Afternoon

Leave Nocé on the D9, stopping for a glimpse of the handsome **Manoir de Courboyer** before spectacular vistas open up along the route. Turn right onto the D5 to the huge, incongruous **Chapelle-Montligeon**. After a look, follow the road through the village until it meets the D213. Turn left through the **Forêt de Réno-Valdieu** *(see p66)* to Monceaux and the glorious **Manoir de Pongirard** gardens (open May–Oct: pm Sat–Sun). Take the D291 to St-Victor-de-Réno for a well-deserved meal at the charming **Auberge de Brochard**.

Around Southern Normandy

Left **Sées Cathedral** Right **Grande Cascade, Mortain**

Towns and Villages

1 Sées
A bishopric since the 4th century, Sées has its fair share of religious buildings: a Gothic cathedral with a very fine interior, a former Bishop's Palace and an abbey. ✆ *Map E5 • Tourist office: pl du Général-de-Gaulle 02 33 28 74 79*

2 St-Céneri-le-Gérei
Not just pretty but officially so (listed as one of France's top 100), this small stone village above the River Sarthe is a little gem which has inspired generations of artists *(see p62).* ✆ *Map E6*

3 L'Aigle
Traditionally a metalworking area, the town plays host each Tuesday to Normandy's biggest market *(see p58).* St Martin's church and the château are both worth a visit. ✆ *Map H5 • Tourist office: pl Fulbert de Beina 02 33 24 12 40*

4 Camembert
Popularized by Napoleon III, the famous cheese was first made here by Marie Harel around 1790. Some nearby farms still use her original method. ✆ *Map E4 • La Ferme "President": 02 33 36 06 60. Open for visits Mar–Oct: daily. Adm charge*

5 Argentan
Apart from its role at the end of the Battle of Normandy (1944), commemorated by the nearby Mémorial de Montormel, the town is known for lace and for horse racing. ✆ *Map E5 • Tourist office: pl du Marché 02 33 67 12 48*

6 Mortagne-au-Perche
Sometime regional capital, and an excellent historic base for exploring, this bustling hill-top town is famous for its black pudding. ✆ *Map H6 • Tourist office: pl de Gaulle 02 33 85 11 18*

7 Bellême
On a rocky spur overlooking forest, vestigial fortifications nestle among well-preserved 17th- and 18th-century houses. There's a wonderful mushroom fair here in late September. ✆ *Map H6 • Tourist office: av Roger Martin du Gard 02 33 73 09 69*

8 Domfront
Perched above the Varenne Gorge, with open views over the pear orchards of the Passais bocage, the ramparts and towers are evidence of the town's turbulent history. ✆ *Map D5 • Tourist office: pl de la Roirie 02 33 38 53 97*

9 Mortain
Mortain is surrounded by woods, waterfalls and granite. Two remarkable falls (Grande and Petite Cascade) are within walking distance of the town centre. ✆ *Map C5 • Tourist office: rue du Bourg Lopin 02 33 59 19 74*

10 Pontorson
Pontorson is something of a gateway to Mont-St-Michel. Its 12th-century church is a fine example of Norman Romanesque. ✆ *Map B5 • Tourist office: pl de l'Hôtel de Ville 02 33 60 20 65*

Left **Musée des Sapeurs-Pompiers de l'Orne** Right **La Ferme du Cheval de Trait**

🔟 Unusual Places to Visit

1 Ecomusée du Moulin de la Sée, Brouains
Admire the giant waterwheel that drove the machinery of this former paper mill on the River Sée. ⊗ *2 le Moulin de Brouains • Map C5 • 02 33 59 50 60 • Open Apr–Sep: daily • Adm charge*

2 Musée Départemental des Sapeurs-Pompiers de l'Orne, Bagnoles-de-l'Orne
A collection of fire pumps and equipment traces the history of French fire-fighting. ⊗ *16 blvd Albert-Christophle • Map D5 • 02 33 38 10 34 • Open Apr–Oct: pm daily • Adm charge*

3 Musée de la Dame aux Camélias, Gacé
The heroine of Alexandre Dumas *fils*'s novel and play lived extravagantly in the Orne. This museum evokes her life. ⊗ *Château de Gacé • Map F5 • 02 33 67 08 59 • Open Jun–Aug: 2–5pm Tue–Sat • Adm charge*

4 Église Saint Julien, Domfront
Built of concrete in 1926, this church boasts Neo-Byzantine-style mosaics. A bomb destroyed the cupola in 1944. ⊗ *pl du Commerce • Map D5 • Open 12 Apr–31 Oct: daily*

5 Le Palais de la Miniature, Les Barils
In Claude Alexandre's fascinating world of miniature soldiers, each figure is hand-crafted. ⊗ *Map H5 • Open Jul–Aug: 11am–12:30pm, 2:30–6pm Tue–Sun; Sep–Jun: phone 02 32 37 64 70 to arrange a visit • Adm charge*

6 La Ferme du Cheval de Trait, Juvigny-sous-Andaine
See horse-drawn agricultural equipment, a miniature farm and displays by Percheron draught-horses. ⊗ *La Michaudière • Map D6 • 02 33 38 27 78 • Displays Jul–Aug: Wed, Thu, Sat & Sun (phone for times) • Adm charge*

7 Musée de l'Emmigration Percheronne au Canada, Tourouvre
A replica of the room where 17th-century locals signed emigration contracts for Québec. ⊗ *15 rue Mondrel • Map H5 • 02 33 25 55 55 • Open Jun–Oct: 11am–6pm Tue–Sun • Adm charge*

8 Musée de Tinchebray et Prison Royale, Tinchebray
A chilling place, with court room, cells and a riveting ethnographic museum. ⊗ *32 Grande Rue • Map D5 • 02 33 64 23 55 • Open Jul–Aug: 2:30–6pm Wed, Thu, Sat & Sun • Adm charge*

9 La Roche d'Oëtre, St-Philbert-sur-Orne
France's oldest mountain – over 2 billion years old – has hiking paths, an exhibition space and a restaurant. ⊗ *Map D5 • 02 31 59 13 13 • www.roche-doetre.fr • Open Feb–Mar: pm Tue–Sun; Apr–Aug: daily; closed in winter • Adm charge*

10 La Maison du Camembert, Camembert
Dedicated to Normandy's famous cheese, with a reconstruction of an old production plant. ⊗ *Le Bourg • Map F4 • 02 33 12 10 37 • Open May–Aug: daily; Sep–Oct: Wed–Sun • Adm charge*

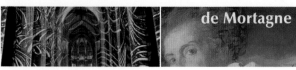

de Mortagne

Left **Les Musilumières de Sées** Right **Les Musicales de Mortagne**

🔟 Cultural Events

1 Septembre Musical de l'Orne
Churches, abbeys and châteaux of the Orne provide the settings for a varied programme including opera, chamber music, jazz and dance. ◎ 02 33 80 44 26 • www.septembre-musical.com • Sep: Fri–Sun

2 Les Musilumières de Sées
The latest technology is used in the sound-and-light show at this romantic 13th-century Gothic cathedral (see p110). ◎ Map E5 • Sées tourist office: 02 33 28 74 79 • Jul–mid-Sep: Fri–Sat

3 Les Hivernales, Falaise
The birthplace of William the Conqueror, Falaise celebrates Christmas with lights, a craft market, choirs and medieval-themed events in front of the castle. ◎ Map E4 • www.falaise-tourisme.com • early Dec–early Jan

4 Les Médiévales de Domfront
In odd-numbered years, troupes of actors and musicians recreate a medieval festival, with games and a market. ◎ Map D5 • Maison des Associations: 02 33 38 56 66 • www.domfront-medievales.com • Aug

5 Les Mardi et Jeudi du Pin, Le Pin-au-Haras
During the summer months, enjoy the weekly musical presentation of stallions, mares, foals and Norman donkeys, at the prestigious national stud farm (see p108). ◎ Jun–Sep: 3–4pm Tue, Thu

6 Les Estivales d'Avranches
Avranches' summer music festival stages concerts by established performers, as well as running courses for novice musicians and choristers. ◎ Map B5 • Avranches tourist office: 02 33 58 00 22 • mid-Jul

7 Le Marché d'Art, La Perrière
Art dealers and connoisseurs flock to this village, which for two days turns into one big gallery exhibiting works by both unknown and established artists. ◎ Map H6 • Whit Sun & Mon

8 Autour d'un Piano, Château de Carrouges
This fine château makes a marvellous venue for recitals by famous soloists and chamber ensembles. ◎ Map E6 • Office Départemental de la Culture: 02 33 31 90 90 • www.ornetourisme.com • late Jul–Aug

9 Les Musicales de Mortagne
Six chamber concerts by world-class performers are staged in stunning settings in the Perche. ◎ Map H6 • Mortagne tourist office: 02 33 85 11 18 • late Jun–mid-Jul

10 Art dans l'Orne, Château de Serans, Ecouché
During the summer a contemporary art and crafts festival is held at a château near Argentan. ◎ 61150 Ecouché • Map E5 • 02 33 36 69 42 • late May–Sep

Price Categories

For a three course meal for one with half a bottle of wine (or equivalent meal), taxes and extra charges.

€	under €30
€€	€30–€40
€€€	€40–€50
€€€€	€50–€60
€€€€€	over €60

Auberge du Terroir, Servon

🔟 Places to Eat

1 La Grange de Tom, Champeaux

This lovely former farm on the cliffs at Champeaux offers an irresistible view across the bay to Mont-St-Michel. The food, much of it grilled over an open fire, is a mix of traditional and modern. ◈ *40 rte des Falaises • Map B5 • 02 33 61 85 52 • €€*

2 Le Gué du Holme, St-Quentin-sur-le-Homme

An immaculate restaurant offering fresh fish, local farm produce and game *(see p128)*. ◈ *14 rue des Estuaires • Map B5 • 02 33 60 63 76 • Closed Mon, Sat L, Sun D • €€€€*

3 Auberge du Terroir, Servon

A friendly, first-class restaurant-with-rooms in a small village close to Mont-St-Michel. ◈ *Le Bourg • Map B5 • 02 33 60 17 92 • Closed Wed, Sat L • €€*

4 Lion Verd, Putanges-Pont-Ecrepin

This local favourite has a pretty riverside terrace by the bridge over the Orne. Vegetarian dishes always on the menu. ◈ *Map E5 • 02 33 35 01 86 • Closed Sun D except Jul–Aug • €€*

5 Auberge du Moulin, Brouains

Diners enjoy traditional, refined, home-made cuisine in this former industrial mill *(see p131)*. ◈ *4 le Moulin de Brouains • Map C5 • 02 33 59 50 60 • Closed Sun D, Mon, Tue • €€*

6 Hôtel du Dauphin, L'Aigle

This comfortable family-run hotel *(see p129)* in the heart of an active market town offers a choice between a restaurant and a brasserie. ◈ *pl de la Halle • Map H5 • 02 33 84 18 00 • Restaurant closed Sun D (brasserie open daily) • €€*

7 Tribunal, Mortagne-au-Perche

An old, well-appointed inn on a quiet square. The attractive restaurant offers a balanced choice of classical and regional dishes *(see p130)*. ◈ *4 pl du Palais • Map H6 • 02 33 25 04 77 • €€*

8 Le Grand Turc, Bellou-en-Houlme

The social centre of the village, serving fresh local produce, this hotel-restaurant can cope with requests from a cup of coffee to a reception for up to 40 people. ◈ *Map D5 • 02 33 66 00 53 • €*

9 Le Tripot, Avranches

A bright, modern bistro with a youthful style. Dishes can include Parmesan and basil lamb or *foie gras au Calvados*. ◈ *11 rue du Tripot • Map B5 • 02 33 60 59 23 • €€*

10 Chez François, Genêts

This cave-like bistro on the Bay of Mont-St-Michel is famous for its grilled meats and delicious desserts. Limited vegetarian options. Booking required. ◈ *prés de la Mairie • Map B5 • 02 33 70 83 98 • Closed Wed, Thu • €€*

Following pages **Rouen café**

113

STREETSMART

NORMANDY'S TOP 10

Left **Rail tickets** Right **Coaches**

🔟 Getting to Normandy

1 By Air
With few international flights to Normandy, most air travellers fly to Paris and take a train. From the UK, Ryanair flies to Paris-Beauvais and Dinard; easyJet goes to Paris Charles de Gaulle; CityJet flies to Deauville; and Air France operates flights from Lyon to Caen and Rouen. ⊗ www.ryanair. com • www.easyjet.com • www.cityjet.com • www. airfrance.com

2 Fly-drive
Fly-drive deals tend to be better value than independent car rental. They can be booked through airlines, tour operators and travel agents, and sometimes include accommodation. The Travel e-Shop lists a number of companies. ⊗ www.traveleshop.com

3 By Ferry to Cherbourg
Brittany Ferries runs Classic Cruise and High Speed services, sailing to Cherbourg from both Portsmouth and Poole. The voyage length varies: Portsmouth–Cherbourg is 3 hours High Speed only (two crossings per day), while Poole–Cherbourg is 6 hours Classic Cruise and 2.5 hours High Speed (three crossings per day). ⊗ www.brittany-ferries.com

4 By Ferry to Le Havre
The ferry network LD Lines has the monopoly on this route, sailing from Portsmouth – once by day (taking 3 hours 15 minutes) and once by night (8 hours). ⊗ www.ldlines.com

5 By Ferry to Dieppe
Transmanche Ferries operates regular trips to Dieppe from Newhaven. There are two or three ferries a day all year round, and the crossing usually takes about 4 hours. ⊗ www.transmancheferries.com

6 By Ferry to Caen-Ouistreham
Brittany Ferries runs the Portsmouth–Caen route, with four crossings a day. It takes 6 hours on a Classic Cruise ferry, and 4 hours on a High Speed. You step off the ferry in the traditional fishing port of Ouistreham, a short drive from Caen.

7 By River
The most romantic way to arrive in Normandy is from Paris by river. Two companies organize a seven-night Seine cruise from Paris to Honfleur: Viking River Cruises and CrosiEurope Alsace Croisières. Their itineraries differ, but both include stops at Vernon, Rouen and Caudebec. ⊗ www.vikingrivers.com • www.croisiere.com

8 By Rail
The excellent national rail network, SNCF, runs a fast, direct service to Rouen, Le Havre, Caen, Bayeux, Cherbourg and Granville from Paris, which links to other European cities via Eurostar. SNCF also offers rail-drive packages. ⊗ www.sncf.com • www. eurostar.com

9 By Road
The Autoroute de Normandie A13 toll motorway starts in Paris and runs south of the Seine to Caen, from where an extension leads to Bayeux and Cherbourg. Other motorways link Normandy with the northern Channel ports and Brittany. By French law, you must carry ID, a driving licence, and car ownership and insurance details (it's also advisable to take out emergency breakdown cover). You must add headlight beam deflectors to a right-hand drive car, and – by French law – carry a red warning triangle, fire extinguisher, first-aid kit and a yellow reflective jacket.

10 By Coach
The cheapest but least relaxing way to get to Normandy. Eurolines and Intercars run coaches between European cities and Paris; from there, you must use a local bus company to reach your destination – for names and numbers, contact local tourist offices *(see p118)*. ⊗ www.eurolines.fr • www.intercars.fr

Left **Rouen Metro** Middle **Bicycling** Right **Getting around on horseback**

TOP 10 Getting Around Normandy

By Rail
SNCF operates a wide rail network linking the region's major towns and cities. One of the most technically advanced train systems in the world, the service is fast, frequent and punctual (see p116).

By Bus
Bus routes link many of the region's major destinations, although schedules are geared to students and commuters rather than tourists, and there's a reduced service at weekends. Coastal routes tend to be the most reliable. Different companies run the network for each département; details are available from the departmental tourist offices.

By Car
With your own car, you can venture off the beaten track. Depending on the type of road, four speed limits apply: on autoroutes, the usual limit is 130 kph (81 mph); on N or RN roads – dual carriageways – it's 110 kph (68 mph); on local D and minor C and V roads, it's 90 kph (56 mph); lastly, there's a limit of 50 kph (31 mph) in all built-up areas.

Car Rental
All the major rental companies operate in Normandy from airports, railway stations and city centres. Most require drivers to be over 21, with a clean licence. Before booking, look into fly-drive packages (see p116).
⬥ www.avis.com • www.budget.com • www.herz.com • www.europcar.com

City Transport
With the exception of central Rouen's fiendish one-way system, most cities are car-friendly, with plenty of pay-and-display parking and car parks. Public transport is largely reliable, with bus services in all towns and cities. Rouen has a metro, and Caen, a tram system.

Taxis
Note that taxis can only be picked up from taxi ranks (stations de taxi) or summoned by telephone – not hailed on the street. Check that your taxi has a meter before entering. Fares can vary from one département to another.

By Bicycle
With its varied terrain and plentiful back-roads, Normandy is a wonderful region for cycling. You can transport your bike by air, rail or ferry, or you can hire one in most towns and at some railway stations. If you're after a mountain bike, look out for the sign VTT (vélos tout terrain). There are permanent cycle paths throughout the region; details are available from tourist offices and local cycling associations.

By Boat
From Vernon, you can spend three hours sight-seeing on the Seine, with commentary by a trained guide and lunch on a converted 1940s barge. There are similar guided river trips on the Douve and the Taute near Carentan, concentrating on the history, geography and environment of the marshlands. ⬥ www.giverny.org/cruises • Douve: 02 33 21 00 33 • Taute: 02 33 55 18 07

On Foot
Normandy is criss-crossed by hundreds of footpaths graded to suit walkers of all levels. The well-known grande randonnée (GR) trails, marked by red and white stripes, take walkers through some spectacular scenery. The departmental tourist offices provide details and mapping of GR routes in their area, and most tourist offices in larger towns and cities publish a "Circuit du Patrimoine", a suggested city tour covering all the interesting sights.

On Horseback
A charming way to enjoy Normandy, whether it's a riding tour of the Perche or a guided trek across the Bay of Mont-St-Michel. You can explore the Orne driving a simple roulotte – a horse-drawn wagon sleeping up to four people. Tourist offices will provide details.

Left **Tourist office** Right **Newspapers**

Sources of Information

1 ATOUT FRANCE
Based in London, the French Tourist Office provides information about Normandy. The helpful team is available to advise on travel, accommodation, places of interest, parks and gardens and all other tourist attractions in Normandy. See the directory box for contact information.

2 Normandie Memoire
The Normandie Memoire website has information for those wishing to visit the sites of the D-Day landings. ✆ *www. normandiememoire.com*

3 Comité Régional du Tourisme
The Normandy Tourism Board is based in Evreux. Visit its office for maps, guides and information about the region, or view its website *(see 6 below)*. ✆ *Le Doyenné, 14 rue Charles- Corbeau • 02 32 33 79 00*

4 Comité Départemental du Tourisme
Each of Normandy's five *départements* has its own tourist office. All are valuable sources of information on travel and accommodation, cultural, sporting and leisure activities, as well as special interests. Consult them when you are planning your trip. ✆ *Calvados: 8 rue Renoir, 14054 Caen. 02 31 27 90 30*

• *Eure: 3 rue du Commdt Letellier, B.P. 367, Evreux. 02 32 62 04 27* • *Manche: Maison du Département, rte de Villedieu, 50008 St-Lô. 02 33 05 98 70* • *Orne: 88 rue St-Blaise, 61002 Alençon. 02 33 28 88 71* • *Seine-Maritime: 6 rue Couronné, 76420 Bihorel. 02 35 12 10 10*

5 Local Tourist Offices
All cities and most towns have a state-run tourist office. Some smaller towns and villages have a private Syndicat d'Initiative (SI). You'll also find multilingual information desks at main railway stations.

6 Websites
The regional tourist office and each of the five departmental tourist offices all have useful websites; note that only those for Normandy and Manche are currently available in English. ✆ *www.normandy-tourism. org • www.calvados-tourisme.com • www.eure-tourisme.fr • www.manche tourisme.com • www.orne tourisme.com • www.seine-maritime-tourisme.com*

7 Public Libraries
Public libraries are found all over Normandy, and they are free. Most have a range of newspapers and magazines, as well as useful notices on activities and events. Only local residents, however, can borrow material.

8 Newspapers
The *International Herald Tribune*, published daily in Paris, is available on day of publication. The pick of the local French papers are *Ouest-France* – a daily with separate departmental editions – and *Paris Normandie*.

9 Television
Most hotels subscribe to multilingual cable and satellite channels, which vary the diet of French-language broadcasting.

10 Radio
If the reception is good enough, you can listen to *Voice of America*, which broadcasts on 1197 kHz AM, or the BBC World Service and BBC for Europe on 648 kHz AM.

French Tourist Offices

Australia
25 Bligh St, Level 13, Sydney NSW 2000
• 02 9231 6277

France
79/81 rue de Clichy, 75009 Paris

United Kingdom
Lincoln House, 300 High Holborn, London • 020 7061 6600 • www. franceguide.com

USA
825 Third Ave, 29th Floor, New York, NY 10022
• 212 838 7800

Left **Mont-St-Michel in summer** Right **Outdoor café tables**

🔟 Things to Avoid

1 Motoring Offences

Police issue heavy fines on the spot for speeding and for other motoring offences. The blood-alcohol limit for drink-driving is low: one glass of wine or a 33 cl bottle of beer will take you close to the limit, two will exceed it. Drivers who cannot pay fines in cash on the spot have their vehicles impounded.

2 Hotel Telephones

Many hotels charge very high rates for international phone calls. It is far cheaper to call from a post office or telephone booth using coins, a credit card or phonecard (see p123).

3 August and Weekends

Like many other European destinations, Normandy is at its best in late spring and early autumn. In August, the seaside resorts are packed with French holidaymakers, and the autoroutes (motorways) become very crowded – especially during the first and last weekends of the month. Resorts are also busy at weekends from spring to autumn, packed with Parisians escaping the city.

4 Queues

Get to popular tourist attractions such as Mont-St-Michel (see pp8–11), Giverny (see pp34–37), the Bayeux Tapestry (see pp12–15), Le Mémorial de Caen (see p25) and Cité de la Mer (see p52) before they open: 15 minutes waiting then could save you much longer queueing time later on. Late afternoon is also a good time to avoid the queues.

5 School Parties

Normandy has always been a very popular destination for both French and English school trips, with the Bayeux Tapestry, D-Day beaches (see pp28–31) and the Mémorial de Caen at the top of the agenda. Though the museums are adept at dealing with them, the resultant noise and high spirits can be distracting, so term-times are best avoided.

6 Mont-St-Michel in Summer

The crowds at Mont-St-Michel in July and August make it quite unbearable. If at all possible, you should try to visit this unique and wonderful site out of season (September to April).

7 Disappointment at Cité de la Mer

Cherbourg's Cité de la Mer has been such a success that, in high season, some visitors are unable to tour the submarine, which can only accommodate a few at a time. In July and August, arrive early to avoid disappointment.

8 Hidden Charges in Cafés and Bars

When paying a bill, make sure you check if service is included – you will usually find that it is. Taking your drink or snack at the counter, if there is one, will be cheaper; prices are lower and no tip is expected – though you could leave some small change if you want to. If you sit at a table, you will be charged for the privilege.

9 Over-tipping

Restaurants and cafés normally include a 10–15 per cent service charge on the bill, so you should only leave a further small gratuity if you feel the service has been particularly good. Taxi drivers should get 15–20 per cent. Porters are tipped €1.50 per bag, and chambermaids a similar amount per day at the end of your stay.

10 Tourist Traps

It used to be said that you could never eat badly in France; sadly, it is becoming increasingly common. Although they are still in the minority, there are more and more places which look for a quick profit at the expense of the tourist, who will in all likelihood never return. Avoid signs proclaiming a "Menu Touristique" – such restaurants may be absolutely fine but, as ever, the best advice is to go where the locals go.

Left **Menu** Middle **Cider** Right **Cheese**

🔟 Eating and Drinking Tips

1 Menus
Most restaurants have several set menus (menu prix-fixe), as well as *à la carte*, from which you order separate dishes. By law, menus must be displayed outside the restaurant. Set menus, which may include wine, are usually excellent value, the cheapest often costing as little as €7.00.

2 Regional Cuisine
The real French eating experience is becoming increasingly elusive; the tinned, the frozen, the bottled and the re-heated are now far too common. However, if you look carefully and avoid tourist traps, you will find in Normandy a great deal of honest cooking using fresh local ingredients. Famous regional dishes, such as *teurgoule* and *poulet Vallée d'Auge (see p54)*, hold sway, and even go-ahead young chefs base their creations on classic Norman dishes. When choosing a restaurant, don't be seduced by a picturesque building; look at the menu first.

3 Wine and Cider
Normandy is too fertile for the grape; any wine you drink will be from another region of France. Cider and *poiré* (pear cider) are often preferred to accompany the rich and creamy regional cuisine. Most cider is sold in a corked bottle (*cidre bouché*).

4 Water
Water is always drunk with meals. Even in up-market restaurants it's acceptable to ask for a *carafe d'eau* (jug of tap water) rather than a bottle of mineral water.

5 Choosing Cheese
Cheese-makers apply the same term as wine-makers to their finest products: AOC *(appellation d'origine contrôlée)*. The most famous Norman cheeses – Camembert, Livarot, Pont l'Evêque and Neufchâtel – are all AOC, but there are more than 30 other types made by local producers.

6 Bloody, Rare or Well Done
If you like your steak well done, order it *bien cuit*; medium, *à point*; rare, *saignant* (bleeding); very rare, *bleu* (blue).

7 Picnics
Like all French people, the Normans love a picnic, so when you plan an al-fresco lunch at the beach or in the country, you will be spoilt for choice. *Boulangeries* (bakeries) and *pâtisseries* (pastry shops) offer a wonderful selection of loaves, pastries, and sweet and savoury tarts. Markets are another good source, with artisan food producers selling farm-made cheeses, *andouilles*, terrines, *tartes aux pommes*, *teurgoules*, and locally produced cider.

8 Vegetarians
Vegetarians are poorly served in Norman restaurants. Few offer anything more than salad, omelette or cheese – soups almost always contain meat stock. However, vegetarians catering for themselves will find mouth-watering fresh fruit and vegetables, delicious cheeses and a wide variety of dairy products. Fish-eaters will have no problems, especially on the coast.

9 Cafés and Bars
There's not much to choose in Normandy between establishments calling themselves cafés and those which call themselves bars. All serve alcoholic drinks and coffee all day, and most serve simple snacks such as ham, cheese or salami sandwiches and perhaps a slice of apple tart. Village cafés usually close around 8pm; city and resort café-bars stay open much later.

10 Bills and Tipping
In cafés, the bill for each drink is brought to your table with your order, but there is no need to pay until you leave. In restaurants, menu prices normally include the service charge; an extra 5 to 10 per cent gratuity for good service is optional *(see p119)*.

Left **Market** Right **Antiques shop**

🔟 Shopping Tips

1 Shopping Hours
Food shops tend to open from 9am to 7 or 8pm Monday–Saturday, with a lunch break from noon to 2pm. Non-food shops generally open 9am–6pm Monday–Saturday. Hypermarkets, supermarkets, department stores and shops in city centres and tourist towns stay open over lunch; others may take a break. Smaller shops may close one day a week, usually Monday. Most shops are closed on Sunday.

2 Taxes and Allowances
If you live within the EU, there are no limits on the amount of wine, spirits, tobacco and perfume you can take home. For non-EU residents, restrictions apply. Non-EU residents can claim back the value added tax (TVA) on purchases worth more than €305 in one shop, as long as they are to be exported within six months.

3 Day Shopping Trips
The Channel ports, especially Dieppe, Le Havre and Cherbourg, are popular destinations for day-trippers from England, mostly intent on buying wine and beer in hypermarkets near the ferry terminals. A website, *www.day-tripper.net*, has full details, but check the sites of ferry companies, too *(see p116)*.

4 Centre Ville, Centre Commercial
The town centre – *centre ville* – is often pedestrianized and full of individual food stores, boutiques and gift shops, ideal for leisurely browsing. At the other end of the spectrum is the *centre commercial* on the outskirts of town, where you will find vast hypermarkets selling everything from food to garden furniture.

5 Markets
One of the great joys of visiting Normandy is shopping in the superb weekly morning markets *(marchés)* that really bring country towns to life. Arrive early to be sure of the best choice; most end at noon. Look out for the specialist local producers with only one or two lines – perhaps cheese or foie gras. Their goods are often high in quality, relatively low in price. Tourist offices can supply a calendar of market days in the area.

6 Vente Directe
All over Normandy, especially in the Pays d'Auge *(see pp32–3)*, you will see roadside signs advertising *vente directe* (direct selling) and *dégustation* (tasting) of home-made produce – commonly cheese, cider and Calvados, but also, for example, foie gras and honey. Usually prices are much lower than in the shops.

7 Regional Produce
Apart from cider, Calvados and cheese *(see p55)*, look out for other local specialities: superb home-made jams, *confiture de lait* (a kind of milk jam), *sablés d'Asnelles* (a shortbread) and *sucres de pomme* ("apple sugars"– a type of bonbon) to mention just a few.

8 Fairs and Festivals
If you're interested in buying local specialities, check with the tourist office to see if one of Normandy's special food-related markets, fairs or festivals is taking place nearby. These include: black pudding (Mortagne), mussels (Le Tréport), cherries (Vernon), cheese (Livarot, Neufchâtel-en-Bray), prawns (Honfleur) and herrings (Dieppe, Fécamp, Étretat).

9 Antiques, Arts and Crafts
Normandy has many antiques and bric-à-brac shops in picturesque towns. Arts and crafts can be found in many specialist shops and craft centres *(see pp64–5)*.

10 Clothes
Normandy is close to Paris, and good clothes are never far away. Caen and Rouen are noted for boutiques and department stores; Deauville, where the *beau monde* flock, is like a miniature version of the rue Faubourg St-Honoré in Paris.

For the best markets See pp58–59

Left **Rouen metro carnet** Right **Jardin des Plantes, Rouen**

TOP10 Normandy on a Budget

1 Off-season Travel
The price of ferry tickets and many hotels, particularly those near the sea, rises in high season. To cut costs, try to avoid visiting Normandy during the summer.

2 Rail Passes
Everybody is eligible for SNCF's value-for-money France Railpass, which allows from three to nine days' travel on any route across France, within one month. The Senior France Railpass for over-60s is valid for groups of up to eight travelling first class. Under-26s are eligible for the France Youthpass (four days' travel over two months), Youth Flexipass (15 days' travel over two months) and Eurailpass (one to two months' unlimited travel).

3 Carnets
If you're planning to stay for some time in a city such as Caen, Le Havre or Rouen, buy a carnet of ten bus (or, in Rouen, metro) tickets – cheaper than buying them individually.

4 Discounts
Most of Normandy's museums and attractions offer cheap admission to students, under-18s and over-60s with ID. The Normandie Pass (€1) entitles the holder to discounted admission to many historical sites and museums in the area.

5 Markets
Even small towns and villages in Normandy have a weekly market. These are excellent places to find affordable food, clothing and bric-à-brac, as well as being colourful and fun.

6 Churches
Not only are they free to visit, some churches and cathedrals also stage free (or very inexpensive) concerts, often during one of the seasonal music festivals (see pp72, 112). Tourist offices will provide details.

7 Camping
Camping is very popular in Normandy, and there are hundreds of campsites to choose from. Most are open from April to October only (some just in high summer). Few sites are near cities, so reaching them without a car may be difficult. Information is available from tourist offices, France Camping EU and Gîtes de France, which run the Camping à la Ferme (camping on the farm) scheme. ✆ www.france-camping.eu.com • www.gites-de-france.fr

8 Budget Accommodation
Fermes auberges and chambres d'hôtes offer exceptionally good value (see p125); alternatively, there are youth hostels, known in France as auberges de jeunesse, in Caen, Dieppe, Vernon and Cherbourg. You don't have to be young to stay in one, but you do need a Hostelling International (HI) card, available from any official youth hostel. For more information, contact the Fédération Unie des Auberges de Jeunesse (FUAJ). For inexpensive hotels, see p131. ✆ FUAJ • 01 44 89 87 27 • www.fuaj.org

9 Free Sights
Many of the best sights in Normandy are free. A short list of suggestions: walk the ramparts at Mont-St-Michel (see p8); visit Rouen Cathedral (see p20–21) and the nearby Aître St-Maclou (see p22); explore the narrow cobbled streets of Honfleur (see pp16–17); stroll along the glamorous boardwalk at Deauville (see p26); go to the bustling Tuesday market at L'Aigle (see p58); ramble in any of the region's forests or parks.

10 Cheap Eats
For a drink or snack, standing at the bar is cheaper than sitting down. In restaurants, the prix-fixe (fixed-price) menus, plat du jour (dish of the day), eau robinet (tap water) and wine or cider by the pichet (jug) offer best value. If you are itching to eat in a gourmet restaurant, go for lunch, when there is usually a cheaper menu.

SNCF rail passes are available at major French railway stations, or can be booked through a travel agent before you leave home.

Left **Euro notes** Middle **A post office sign** Right **Public phone booth**

TOP 10 Banking & Communications

1 Currency

Since January 2002, the euro has been the official currency in France. Euro banknotes have seven denominations: 5, 10, 20, 50, 100, 200 and 500. There are also eight coin denominations: €1 and €2, and 1, 2, 5, 10, 20 and 50 cents.

2 Changing Money

You can exchange foreign currency and travellers' cheques for euros at banks, bureaux de change, American Express offices and some post offices. Check exchange rates before you travel. In bureaux de change, check that the rate offered and the commission charged are reasonable. Avoid changing money in hotels.

3 ATMs

Most towns have ATMs (automatic teller machines) – a convenient way of drawing cash from your bank or credit card account. Each one indicates which cards it accepts. Many function in several languages.

4 Credit and Debit Cards

Major cards are widely accepted throughout Normandy, and you should have no difficulty paying for most things – motorway tolls included – with plastic. Smaller shops, restaurants, hotels, campsites and *gîte* operators prefer cash.

5 Travellers' Cheques

Travellers' cheques can be exchanged for cash in banks, and are widely accepted in retail outlets. Choose a well-known company like American Express or Thomas Cook.

6 Post Offices

French post offices, easily identifiable by their yellow and blue "La Poste" sign, open 9am–noon and 2–5pm Monday to Friday, and Saturday mornings. You can buy stamps in *tabacs* (tobacconists), as well as post offices.

7 Fax and Poste Restante

Faxes can be sent or received at all post offices. Main post offices will hold mail addressed to individuals on the move until collected in person. The envelope should carry the recipient's name (surname first), the words "poste restante", and the address of the post office, including the five-digit postal code. The person collecting the mail needs to take ID and pay a small fee.

8 Language and Etiquette

English is widely spoken by people in the Channel ports, cities and main towns, but less so in rural Normandy, where you will need a grasp of French to understand and be understood. Meeting and greeting is an art form: hand-shaking is *de rigueur* when you are introduced to someone, and between acquaintances. It is polite to acknowledge people formally: "Bonjour, madame/monsieur".

9 Telephones

With telephone cards (*télécartes*), which may be purchased in all post offices, newsagent's shops and *tabacs*, you can make both local and international calls from any public telephone booth. The *pays direct* service enables you to call via an operator in your own country, and pay by debit or credit card. To call France from abroad, dial the relevant international code followed by 33, then the number (omitting the first zero).

10 Internet

Internet cafés are few and far between in Normandy, however Wi-Fi is readily available in many locations, including public buildings. Visitors to the region will find plenty of spots where they can log on to the Internet using their own laptop computer or smart phone. In places such as cafés, it may be necessary to make a purchase in order to obtain Wi-Fi access.

Left **An emergency telephone on a motorway** Right **A *pharmacie* (chemist)**

🔟 Security and Health

1 Emergencies

In a medical emergency, contact the 24-hour Service d'Aide Médicale Urgence, which can send a doctor, an ambulance, or paramedics in a mobile intensive care unit, as appropriate. For all but the most serious emergencies, payment in cash is required immediately after treatment. ✆ *SOS Médecins 01 47 07 77 77*

2 Travel Insurance

Health care in France is excellent but expensive, so be sure to take out adequate insurance to cover any medical emergency. Visitors from the EU should additionally obtain a European Health Insurance Card (EHIC) online or from a post office before departure.

3 Crime

Generally speaking, Normandy is a pretty safe place to travel; violent crimes, such as assault and rape, are comparatively rare. Most crime involves theft – particularly from cars. Pickpockets and bag-snatchers tend to operate in city centres, usually in crowded places like railway stations, trains and buses, and bars and clubs. If you are unlucky enough to have anything stolen, report it to the nearest police station straight away, and ask for a copy of the police report for your insurers.

4 Breakdowns and Car Accidents

If your car breaks down, wear your yellow reflective jacket *(see p116)* and – walking behind the barrier for safety – place the red warning triangle 50–100 m (160–300 ft) behind it. If you have an accident, telephone the emergency services *(see box)*. Postes d'appel d'urgence (emergency telephones) are posted at 2 km (1 mile) intervals on *autoroutes*, 4 km (2.5 miles) on dual carriageways; they will connect you with rescue services via the traffic police.

5 Pharmacies

Pharmacies (chemists) – indicated by a green cross – are usually very helpful for minor ailments and injuries. If necessary, they will also direct you to the nearest doctor. Normal opening hours are 8 or 9am–7pm Monday to Saturday, but one pharmacy in every town stays open at night and weekends; others will post the address on their doors.

6 Hospitals

If you have an accident or fall ill in the night, go to any public hospital's *service des urgencies* (accident-and-emergency department). Be warned: you must pay for your treatment straight away.

7 Doctors

If you are staying in a hotel, staff should be able to recommend an English-speaking doctor, or put you in touch with the 24-hour *médecin de garde* (doctor service) that operates in every major town. If not, consult your local pharmacist or the telephone operator.

8 Dentists

Dentists are listed in local Pages Jaunes (Yellow Pages). In an emergency, they will see you at major hospitals.

9 Documents

Always carry some form of identification with you, and have your driving licence, insurance and car registration documents to hand when driving. If you are stopped by the police, failure to produce them may result in an on-the-spot fine.

10 Lost Passport

If you lose your passport, report it to the police immediately. Next, inform your embassy or consulate; most are in Paris, but some are based in Rouen. Make copies of all your important documents and keep them separately.

Emergency Phone Numbers

Switchboard
112

Police
17

Ambulance
15

Fire Brigade
18

Left *Gîtes* sign Middle **Camping** Right **A hotel in the Formule 1 chain**

⑩ Accommodation Tips

1 High and Low Season

If you plan on visiting Normandy in high season, whether you want to stay in a grand hotel or on a campsite, it would be wise to book well ahead. Normandy is a popular destination from spring to autumn, but from early July to late August the resorts in particular are at their busiest. This is especially true of Deauville during its August season, and weekends throughout the year are always very busy there. Some smaller hotels in rural areas close from November to March.

2 How to Book

You can book accommodation direct by phone, fax or, increasingly, by e-mail and via the web; *www.normandy-tourism. org* provides useful links. Sometimes a deposit may be required; in large hotels and campsites, you can usually pay by credit card or by money order.

3 Families

Normandy is particularly well geared to family tourism, both on the coast and inland. Many hotels will provide an extra bed for smaller children, or a cot for babies, at a nominal cost. *Gîtes (see p133)* and campsites *(see p132)* also offer excellent value for families travelling on a budget. Most campsites have facilities and activities for children.

4 On a Budget

Hotels in France can be surprisingly good value *(see p131)*. *Fermes auberges* and *chambres d'hôtes (see below)* are also sources of inexpensive accommodation. The best way to save money is to travel off-season.

5 Bed and Breakfast

Accommodation in private homes *(chambres d'hôtes)*, from simple to stately, is available across Normandy. Owners who belong to the Fédération Nationale des Gîtes Ruraux de France are regularly inspected; accommodation is usually in rural areas *(www.gites-de-france-normandie.com)*. Urban B&Bs are handled by Clévacances *(www. clevacances.com)*. *Fermes auberges* are working farms with simple restaurants and a few bedrooms. For details, visit *www.normandieala ferme.com* or contact the relevant local tourist office *(see p118)*.

6 Camping

Campsites vary from small establishments in unspoilt countryside to large, well-equipped sites close to towns, with pools, café-bars and, often, a mini-market and morning bread delivery. They become crowded in July and August, and most close their gates by 10pm. Independent camping is discouraged, as is sleeping on beaches.

7 Hotel Chains

France pioneered the "limited service hotel" offering clean, comfortable rooms at budget prices. Chains such as Formule 1, Etap and Campanile cluster at motorway junctions and airports, and on the outskirts of cities. Though lacking in character, they can be ideal for the first and last nights of your stay. A more attractive option is Logis de France *(www.logis-de-france.fr)*.

8 Relais et Châteaux

The hotels in the Relais et Châteaux group are independently owned, but they are all expected to measure up to high standards of food, service and accommodation. The buildings in which they are located are of historic importance. ✆ *www. relaischateaux.com*

9 Self-catering

Accommodation in *gîtes* is plentiful. Often they are pretty cottages or farmhouses – most of them privately owned. Crockery and kitchen utensils are supplied, but you have to bring your own bed linen and do your own cleaning *(see p133)*.

10 Apartments

Holiday apartments can be found in resort areas, particularly along the Côte Fleurie between Deauville and Cabourg. Few offer the facilities of a *gîte*, and most are geared to long stays.

Left **France et des Fuchsias, St-Vaast-la-Hougue** Right **La Terrasse, Varengville-sur-Mer**

🔟 Seaside Hotels

1 France et des Fuchsias, St-Vaast-la-Hougue

Perennially popular with yachtsmen and Cherbourg ferry passengers, this captivating little hotel puts its main emphasis on the restaurant, which serves marvellous seafood platters. The best bedrooms are in the annexe overlooking the delightful English-style garden. ✪ 20 rue Maréchal Foch • Map B2 • 02 33 54 40 41 • www.france-fuchsias.com • €

2 Hôtel Le Central, Trouville-sur-Mer

Facing the fishing port of this resort, Le Central has 23 spacious rooms decorated in calming neutral tones with great harbour views. Amenities include in-room Wi-Fi. Golf courses and casinos are located nearby. ✪ 5–7 rue des Bains • Map E3 • 02 31 88 80 84 • www.le-central-trouville.com • €€€

3 Hôtel de la Marine, Barneville-Carteret

La Marine is well known for its Michelin-starred restaurant with splendid views over the harbour, but since it is close to all the superb beaches of the Cotentin Peninsula's west coast, it also makes a good base for a seaside holiday. Ask for a room with a sea view. ✪ 11 rue de Paris • Map A3 • 02 33 53 83 31 • www.hotel marine.com • Closed mid-Dec–mid-Feb • €€€

4 La Marine, Arromanches

On the seafront opposite the D-Day Musée du Débarquement, this is a popular base for visiting the landing beaches. It has a pleasant seafood restaurant, simple bedrooms and an unfussy, old-fashioned air. ✪ 1 quai du Canada • Map D3 • 02 31 22 34 19 • www.hotel-de-la-marine.fr • €€

5 Duguesclin, Grandcamp-Maisy

The friendly and efficient Duguesclin is the best place to stay in this little fishing port in the midst of the D-Day landing beaches. ✪ 4 quai Henri-Crampon • Map C3 • 02 31 22 64 22 • €

6 Hôtel des Ormes, Barneville-Carteret

The ultimate seaside hotel in Normandy, this charmingly decorated establishment sits right on the beach. It offers a fine restaurant, a tranquil garden and lovely views over the boats in the marina. ✪ prom Barbey-d'Aurevilly • Map A3 • 02 33 52 23 50 • www.hoteldes-ormes.com • €€€

7 Le Flaubert, Trouville-sur-Mer

Situated on the beach, the Flaubert is a glorious place to stay in Trouville, one of the birthplaces of Impressionism. ✪ rue Gustave Flaubert • Map E3 • 02 31 88 37 23 • www.flaubert.fr • €€€–€€€€

8 L'Augeval, Deauville

In the heart of Deauville, a short distance from the casino, boutiques and glitzy seafront boardwalk, is the delightful Augeval. Comprised of two listed Anglo-Norman-style villas, the rooms have spa baths and there is a heated pool in the grounds. ✪ 15 av Hocquart de Turtot • Map E3 • 02 31 81 13 18 • www.augeval.com • €€€–€€€€€

9 Dormy House, Étretat

With an Art Deco-style main building and two (rather more comfortable) annexes, this hotel sits amongst greenery, with fine views over the town, the sea and Étretat's famous cliffs, Falaises d'Aval and d'Amont. ✪ rte Le Havre • Map G2 • 02 35 27 07 88 • www.dormy-house.com • €€

10 La Terrasse, Varengville-sur-Mer

A narrow lane winds through typical Norman countryside to the cliff-edge and this characterful small hotel, with wooden balconies. The 22 rooms are homely, the atmosphere welcoming. There are magical sea views from the covered terrace (where meals are served in summer). ✪ Vasterival • Map J1 • 02 35 85 12 54 • www.hotel-restaurant-la-terrasse.com • Closed mid-Oct–mid-Mar • €€

Unless otherwise stated, all hotels accept credit cards and have en-suite bathrooms and air-conditioning.

Price Categories

For a standard, double room per night (with breakfast if included), taxes and extra charges.

€ under €60
€€ €60–€100
€€€ €100–€150
€€€€ €150–€250
€€€€€ over €250

La Ferme St-Siméon, Honfleur

🔟 Luxury Hotels

1 La Ferme St-Siméon, Honfleur
This ancient farmhouse on the Seine estuary, once a meeting place of Impressionist painters, is now the most luxurious – and expensive – country hotel in Normandy. 🆂 rue A-Marais • Map F3 • 02 31 81 78 00 • www.fermesaint simeon.fr • €€€€€

2 L'Absinthe, Honfleur
L'Absinthe, close to the Vieux Port, is the most intimate hotel in Honfleur, with seven well-equipped, beamed bedrooms, a restaurant, a brasserie and a cosy, wood-panelled reception room. 🆂 10 quai de la Quarantaine • Map F3 • 02 31 89 23 23 • www. absinthe.fr • Closed mid-Nov–mid-Dec • €€€

3 Normandy Barrière, Deauville
With its rambling timber-framed façade, the Normandy has the air of a quaint Norman cottage built for a giant. Inside, there are chandeliers and columns, an indoor swimming pool around which breakfast can be served, and a handy underground passage leading to the Casino – which happens to belong to the same hotel and leisure group (it also owns Bar de la Mer and Bar du Soleil on the seafront promenade). 🆂 38 rue Mermoz • Map E3 • 02 31 98 66 22 • www.normandy-barriere.com • €€€€€

4 Royal Barrière, Deauville
With its grand hall dressed strikingly in red, its glamorous panelled restaurant, and its outdoor swimming pool and terrace, the Royal is the perfect Deauville hotel for anyone who wishes to see and be seen. Discreet; no; flashy and fun, yes. 🆂 blvd Cornuché • Map E3 • 02 31 98 66 33 • www.lucien barriere.com • €€€€€

5 Grand Hôtel Mercure, Cabourg
Celebrated for its association with Marcel Proust, who spent his childhood holidays here and famously described the dining room as an aquarium, this huge white edifice is still redolent of its *belle époque* heyday, with vast rooms and balconies. The front faces the town, while the rear opens onto the beach. 🆂 prom Marcel-Proust • Map E3 • 02 31 91 01 79 • www.accorhotels. com • €€€

6 Château de la Chenevière, Port-en-Bessin
With 19 suites and one standard room, this elegant 18th-century château standing in its own parkland has the feeling of a gracious English country house. It makes a convenient base for the D-Day beaches and Bayeux. 🆂 Map C3 • 02 31 51 25 25 • www. lacheneviere.com • €€€€

7 Château d'Audrieu, Audrieu
Within easy reach of Bayeux, Caen and the D-Day beaches, this 18th-century château was the family home of the owners until it became a hotel in 1976. Bedrooms are particularly elegant. 🆂 Map D3 • 02 31 80 21 52 • www.chateau daudrieu.com • €€€€€

8 Château de Sully, Bayeux
This cool, handsome hotel has a contemporary feel, sympathetically blending modern comforts with its 18th-century surroundings. 🆂 rte de Port-en-Bessin • Map D3 • 02 31 22 29 48 • www.cha teau-de-sully.com • €€€

9 Château Les Bruyères, Cambremer
In the heart of the Pays d'Auge, this stone-built château makes a luxurious bed-and-breakfast stop along the Cider Route. 🆂 rte du Cadran • Map E4 • 02 31 32 22 45 • www.chateaulesbruyeres. com • €€€€

10 Hôtel Bourgtheroulde, Rouen
This boutique hotel, in a 16th-century building, has a stunning modern atrium bar, restaurant, spa and an illuminated swimming pool. 🆂 15 pl de la Pucelle • Map L5 • 02 35 14 50 50 • www.hotel sparouen.com • €€€€

Left **Auberge de l'Abbaye, Le Bec-Hellouin** Right **Manoir du Butin, Honfleur**

Country Hotels

1 Hôtel de la Licorne, Lyons-la-Forêt

This classic half-timbered inn dating from 1610 offers 14 contemporary rooms, five suites (including one for disabled visitors) and an apartment sleeping up to six people. There is also a fine restaurant *(see p83).* ❧ *27 pl Benserade • Map K3 • 02 32 48 24 24 • www. hotel-licorne.com • €€€*

2 Le Petit Coq aux Champs, Campigny

Helicopters arriving here in the wooded Risle Valley (and some do) look for two thatched roofs joined by a modern extension. The decoration and superb food are also fusions of old and new, and every bedroom has its own character and style. ❧ *400 chemin du Petit Coq • Map H3 • 02 32 41 04 19 • www.lepetit coqauxchamps.fr • €€€*

3 Auberge de l'Abbaye, Le Bec-Hellouin

This half-timbered 18th-century inn with five comfortable, cottage-style bedrooms sits opposite the entrance to the abbey of Notre-Dame du Bec. Run by the same family for more than 40 years, it radiates friendly efficiency and offers meals both formal and informal, inside or out on its terrace. ❧ *pl Guillaume le Conquérant • Map H3 • 02 32 44 86 02 • €€*

4 La Réserve, Giverny

More a luxury B&B than a hotel, La Réserve is the best place to stay when in the Giverny area. Its five sumptuous rooms are full of light and tastefully decorated with beautiful antiques and floral soft furnishings. The charming, personal service adds an extra dimension to a stay here. ❧ *Map K4 • 02 32 21 99 09 • www.giverny-lareserve.com • €€€*

5 Verte Campagne, Trelly

This ivy-festooned 16th-century Norman farmhouse in a peaceful hamlet retains its charming beams and bare stone walls. If the thoughtful, well-presented menus downstairs tempt you to stay overnight, the bedrooms are very comfortable. ❧ *Map B4 • 02 33 47 65 33 • www. lavertecampagne.com • €€*

6 Manoir du Butin, Honfleur

Most of the good-sized rooms in this small, relaxed manor – round the side of a hill, minutes away from the hurly-burly of Honfleur – look out over the Seine estuary. Each room is styled individually, and residents have first call on the attractive restaurant downstairs. ❧ *Phare du Butin • Map F3 • 02 31 81 63 00 • www.hotel-lemanoir.fr • €€€€*

7 Le Gué du Holme, St-Quentin-sur-le-Homme

Michel Leroux is probably the best chef for miles in any direction, and any thought of driving on should be dispelled by the quietly comfortable rooms – most of them in a modern wing overlooking the rose garden. ❧ *14 rue des Estuaires • Map B5 • 02 33 60 63 76 • www.le-gue-du-holme.com • €€*

8 Château de Boucéel, Vergoncey

This lovely 1760s château near the Bay of Mont-St-Michel is run by the descendants of its original owners. Its palatial rooms offer superb value for money. ❧ *Map B5 • 02 33 48 34 61 • www.chateau debouceel.com • €€€*

9 Le Pavillon de Gouffern, Silly-en-Gouffern

To the east of Argentan, this handsome, well-dressed 18th-century hunting lodge is set in its own extensive wooded park at the source of the River Orne. ❧ *Map E5 • 02 33 36 64 26 • www. pavillondegouffern.com • €€*

10 Château de la Rapée, Gisors

A real Gothic mansion at the end of a rutted forest track. Spacious rooms, fine furniture, pleasing views, excellent cooking. ❧ *Bazincourt-sur-Epte • Map K3 • 02 32 55 11 61 • www. hotelrapee.com • €€*

Price Categories

For a standard, double room per night (with breakfast if included), taxes and extra charges.

€	under €60
€€	€60–€100
€€€	€100–€150
€€€€	€150–€250
€€€€€	over €250

Le Dauphin, Caen

🔟 Town Hotels

1 Le Dauphin, Caen
This lovingly restored former priory does not reveal its age until you get inside. Some of the comfortable bedrooms are in the building next door. In the smart dining room, the owner Stéphane Pugnat's food is a highlight. ◎ *29 rue Gémare • Map M2 • 02 31 86 22 26 • www.le-dauphin-normandie.com • €€€*

2 Hôtel d'Argouges, Bayeux
This classically propor-tioned 17th-century town-house is furnished with antiques. Rooms vary in size, but are all decorated in quite good taste with, for the most part, larger-than-average bathrooms. Guests can use the smart, light drawing room and the garden. There is off-street park-ing. ◎ *21 rue St-Patrice • Map D3 • 02 31 92 88 86 • www.ohotellerie.com/dargouges • €€€*

3 Auberge St-Pierre, Mont-St-Michel
The 15th-century *auberge* is one of a handful of hotels at the foot of Mont St-Michel and close to the causeway (useful, since all cars have to be left outside its walls). There is a large, busy restaurant at street level, while on the first floor, a pleasantly rustic calm takes over. ◎ *Grande Rue • Map B5 • 02 33 60 14 03 • www.auberge-saint-pierre.fr • €€€*

4 Hôtel des Loges, Honfleur
Honfleur's latest hotel is an old building with a contemporary interior: quarry-tiled floors, pale cream walls, black-and-white photographs; and in the breakfast room, black iron tables, black wicker chairs and modern lighting. Bedrooms, in a separate building across a courtyard, are very quiet. ◎ *18 rue Brûlée • Map F3 • 02 31 89 38 26 • www.hoteldesloges.com • €€€*

5 Hôtel des Carmes, Rouen
An inexpensive, endearing hotel overlooking a quiet, tree-filled square. The owner is an artist; her paintings and sculptures decorate the ground floor, while the bedrooms are being redecorated in bright colours with her frescoes on the ceilings. ◎ *33 pl des Carmes • Map M5 • 02 35 71 92 31 • www.hoteldescarmes.com • €*

6 Le Normandie, Bagnoles de l'Orne
This handsome old stone-built inn has a highly recommended restaurant. In summer, meals are served in the attractive garden. There is a fine view from the front across wooded countryside and park. ◎ *2 ave du Dr Paul-Lemuet • Map D5 • 02 33 30 71 30 • www.hotel-le-normandie.com • €€*

7 Hôtel Oscar, Le Havre
Decorated throughout in sleek 1950s decor, Hôtel Oscar blends the style of post-war France with modern comforts. It is a fitting retreat after a visit to the D-Day landing sites. ◎ *106 rue Voltaire • Map E2 • 02 35 42 39 77 • www.hotel-oscar.fr • €€*

8 Hôtel Villa Josephine, Deauville
Villa Josephine is a traditional half-timbered house, richly furnished with antiques and velvet drapes. Guests can enjoy the quiet garden or head to the nearby beach for more energetic activities such as horse riding, jet-skiing or windsurfing. ◎ *23 rue des Villas • Map E3 • 02 31 14 18 00 • www.villajosephine.fr • €€€€*

9 Hostellerie Genty-Home, Mortagne-au-Perche
A traditional stone-built inn in the centre of this unspoilt market town. ◎ *4 rue Notre-Dame • Map F6 • 02 33 25 11 53 • €*

10 Hôtel du Dauphin, L'Aigle
This 17th-century *relais de poste* has an excellent restaurant and brasserie, a fine wood-panelled salon, and bedrooms that blend old with new. ◎ *pl de la Halle • Map H5 • 02 33 84 18 00 • www.hotel-dudauphin.free.fr • €€*

Unless otherwise stated, all hotels accept credit cards and have en-suite bathrooms and air-conditioning.

Left **Ferme de la Rançonnière, Crépon** Right **Le Moulin de Connelles, Connelles**

Hotels with Character

1 Ferme de la Rançonnière, Crépon

Early inhabitants of this medieval fortified farm tried to keep people out: the present incumbents are far more welcoming. On Sundays, the two dining rooms only just manage to keep pace with the regulars. The rooms are baronial. *rte d'Arromanches • Map D3 • 02 31 22 21 73 • www. ranconniere.fr • €€€*

2 Château d'Agneaux, St-Lô

This small but perfectly formed 13th-century château looks down on the Vire Valley. The bedrooms are finely furnished, and the flagged dining hall offers excellent regional cuisine. *ave Ste-Marie, Agneaux • Map C4 • 02 33 57 65 88 • www.chateau-agneaux.com • €€€*

3 Le Logis d'Eawy, St-Saëns

Enjoy a relaxing stay at this half-timbered house full of charming, distinctive features. It is the ideal base from which to explore the Forêt d'Eawy (see p66) and the Pays de Bray (see p43). *1 rue du 31 Août • Map J2 • 06 19 15 52 04 • www. logisdeawy.com • €€*

4 Le Moulin de Connelles, Connelles

When you see the turreted mill's reflection between the lily pads that float beneath the restaurant window, you know you are in picture-postcard territory. A small, deeply comforta-ble hotel, with bathrooms to die for and a chef to kill for. *rte d'Amfreville-sous-les-Monts • Map J3 • 02 32 59 53 33 • www. moulin-de-connelles.fr • €€€*

5 Château de Canisy, Canisy

Here's a chance to stay at a heavenly château. Privately owned, it has been in the same family for almost 1,000 years. Set in acres of parkland, it is exquisitely decorated with antique pieces and heirlooms. *6–8 rue Kergorlay • Map C4 • 01 44 05 09 81 • www.canisy. com • €€€€€*

6 Le Manoir des Saules, La Saussaye

Partly timbered, partly chequerboard brick and stone, this typical Norman manor has been lovingly restored to provide 10 restful bedrooms, and public rooms filled with antique furniture and Oriental carpets. *2 pl St-Martin • Map J4 • 02 35 87 25 65 • www.manoirdessaules. com • €€€€*

7 Hôtel d'Outre-Mer, Villers-sur-Mer

At this original boutique-style hotel near the beach every room is decorated in a different colour scheme. In addition to free Wi-Fi connection, the hotel offers a library and board games. Hip but laid-back. *1 rue du Maréchal Leclerc • Map E3 • 02 31 87 04 64 • www. hoteloutremer.com • €€€*

8 Château de Goville, Le Breuil-en-Bessin

Set in rolling countryside, this elegantly furnished 18th-century château has 12 pretty bedrooms over-looking an impeccable jardin à la française. *Map C3 • 02 31 22 19 28 • www.chateaugoville-normandie.com • €€€*

9 Tribunal, Mortagne-au-Perche

Occupying a handsome building with origins in the 13th century, this welcoming central hotel is an excellent base for exploring the Perche (see p113). *4 pl de Palais • Map H6 • 02 33 25 04 77 • www. hotel-tribunal.fr • €€*

10 Moulin de Villeray, Condeau-au-Perche

If you want to inject a lit-tle romance into your life, spend a couple of days at this seductive riverside estate set in the beauti-ful, unspoilt Perche countryside. The rooms, housed in a château and a mill, are full of character. There is also a glorious mature garden to enjoy. *Map H6 • 02 33 73 30 22 • www.domainedevil-leray.com • €€€*

Unless otherwise stated, all hotels accept credit cards and have en-suite bathrooms and air-conditioning.

Price Categories

For a standard, double room per night (with breakfast if included), taxes and extra charges.

€	under €60
€€	€60–€100
€€€	€100–€150
€€€€	€150–€250
€€€€€	over €250

Left **Le Régence, Cherbourg**

TOP 10 Budget Hotels

1 La Régence, Cherbourg
Facing the quay, this popular bistro offers small, plain rooms, some with kitchenettes, in a quiet annexe. It makes a decent base in a town not noted for its hotels. ✪ *42 quai de Caligny • Map B2 • 02 33 43 05 16 • www.laregence.com • €€*

2 La Fossardière, Omonville-la-Petite
This typical old stone building in one of the prettiest villages on the Hague Peninsula has been carefully restored to provide cosy lodgings. Closed mid-November to mid-March. ✪ *Hameau de la Fosse • Map A2 • 02 33 52 19 83 • €€*

3 Auberge du Moulin, Brouains
A tall factory chimney proclaims the utilitarian past of this converted mill. Locals dine here on special occasions; travellers will find five neat bedrooms, with floral bedcovers, modern wall lights and the odd beam. ✪ *4 le Moulin de Brouains • Map C5 • 02 33 59 50 60 • www.aubergedumoulin.net • €*

4 Michelet, Granville
Near the atmospheric old town, this plain, friendly hotel is close to shops, restaurants and casino. ✪ *5 rue Jules-Michelet • Map B5 • 02 33 50 06 55 • €*

5 Central, Caen
This low-cost bed-and-breakfast with 25 basic bedrooms enjoys a convenient location, just a few paces from William the Conqueror's château, which can be seen from some windows. ✪ *23 pl Letellier • Map M2 • 02 31 86 18 52 • www.centralhotel-caen.com • €*

6 Arcades, Rouen
In this friendly tourist hotel, you can choose between a room with shower and WC, shower only, or just a washbasin. Though basic, bedrooms are prettily decorated, with pine furniture. Rue des Carmes is a busy central shopping street between the Palais des Congrès and Palais de Justice, close to the cathedral. ✪ *52 rue des Carmes • Map M5 • 02 35 70 10 30 • www.hotel-des-arcades.com • €*

7 La Cour Ste-Catherine, Honfleur
This charming bed-and-breakfast, close to the old port, is housed in a 17th-century building that used to be a convent. The five rooms (one per floor) are tastefully decorated and feature en-suite bathrooms and DVD players. Nearby are three self-catering apartments that sleep five. Breakfast is included, and there is free Wi-Fi. ✪ *74 rue du Puits • Map F3 • 02 31 89 42 40 • www.coursaintecatherine.com • €€*

8 Logis Les Ramparts, Bayeux
Owned by François Lecornu, the only cider producer within Bayeux town, this charming hotel has bags of character. The rooms are all non-smoking and beautifully decorated with antiques and rich soft furnishings, but no TV set. There's no disabled access. ✪ *4 rue Bourbesneur • Map C3 • 02 31 92 50 40 • www.lecornu.fr • €–€€*

9 Les Agriculteurs, St-Pierre-sur-Dives
This long-established family-run Logis de France in the heart of the Pays d'Auge has a cosy, familial atmosphere, clean, pretty bedrooms and – its focal point – a popular local restaurant serving straightforward regional food. All in all, it's good value. Try to be in St-Pierre-sur-Dives for the wonderful Monday market *(see p59)*. ✪ *118 rue de Falaise • Map E4 • 02 31 20 72 78 • www.lesagriculteurs.com • €*

10 Aux 13 Arches, Portbail
This cool little budget hotel-restaurant is situated right by the seashore in a tiny harbour near Barneville-Carteret. Rooms are simply but tastefully decorated, and they look over a decked area. ✪ *9 pl Castel • Map A3 • 02 33 04 87 90 • www.13arches.com • €€*

Left **Camping de la Vée, Bagnoles-de-l'Orne** Right **Camping de l'Ermitage, Donville-les-Bains**

TOP 10 Campsites

1 Château le Colombier, Moyaux

A traditional, upmarket campsite – with no caravans or bungalows – in the grounds of an elegant Auge château, where (if you book) you can dine on Tuesday and Saturday. It has a heated pool, *crêperie*, bar, grocery, games room and mini golf. No karaoke nights here; instead, they stage open-air classical music recitals. ✆ *Map G3 • 02 31 63 63 08 • www. camping-lecolombier.com • €*

2 Camping des Deux Rivières, Martigny

Hard to believe, but this peaceful campsite tucked away on an island is only a short drive from Dieppe. There are plenty of indoor amusements, but with the Arques Forest, Varenne River and a lake on the doorstep, this is really a place for outdoor types. ✆ *Map J1 • 02 35 85 60 82 • www.camping-2-rivieres.com • Closed mid-Oct–late Mar • €*

3 Château de Lez Eaux, St-Pair-sur-Mer

This four-star campsite offers large, luxury "pitch-es", and wood cabins for five. If you tire of the aquapark, tennis, volley-ball and billiards, Mont-St-Michel, Granville and Brittany beckon. ✆ *Map B5 • 02 33 51 66 09 • www.lez-eaux.com • Closed end Sep–end Mar • €*

4 La Vallée, Houlgate

This very large and well-equipped site is just a short walk from Houlgate beach, where you can take sailing lessons and go sea fishing. ✆ *88 route de la Vallée • Map E3 • 02 31 24 40 69 • www.campinglavallee.com • Closed Oct–Mar • €*

5 Le Ranch, Le Rozel

This Cotentin beach is the place to come for serious surfing. Pitch a tent, or take one of the well-designed caravans. ✆ *Map A2 • 02 33 10 07 10 • www.camping-leranch. com • Closed Oct–Apr • €*

6 Camping du Vievre, St-Georges-du-Vièvre

Most of the campers here are fresh-air fiends, drawn by the prospect of energetic hikes through the countryside or taxing mountain bike rides. If that sounds too much like hard work, there is tennis, table tennis and a pool on site. ✆ *Map H3 • 02 32 42 76 79 • www. camping-eure-normandie.fr • Closed Oct–Apr • €*

7 La Côte de Nacre, St-Aubin-sur-Mer

This family-oriented, four-star campsite has a great swimming pool complex, with water chutes, kids' activities and organized entertainment. ✆ *rue Général Moulton • Map H1 • 02 31 97 14 45 • www. camping-cote-de-nacre.com • Closed Oct–Apr • €*

8 Camping de la Vée, Bagnoles-de-l'Orne

The joy of La Vée is its position – close to Bagnoles *(see pp61)* and the Andaines Forest *(see pp66)*. Its 250 "pitches" are in leafy surroundings, with amenities including a snack bar, and recreation and games rooms. ✆ *5 rue du Président Coty • Map D5 • 02 33 37 87 45 • www. bagnolesdelorne.com • Closed end Nov–Feb • €*

9 Camping de l'Ermitage, Donville-les-Bains

With its own bakery, delicatessen, snack bar and visiting traders, you seldom need to leave this large, well-run camp-site. Close by, you can gather shells on the sandy beach, ride, play tennis, or relax in the thalassotherapy centre (from 2013). ✆ *Map B4 • 02 33 50 09 01 • www.camping-ermitage.com • Closed mid-Oct–mid-Apr • €*

10 Les Gravelets, Montmartin-sur-Mer

This two-star seaside campsite was converted from a lime quarry in 1983. One of the pits is now used for rock climb-ing; the other has been turned into tennis courts. Catch your own seafood and cook it over a camp-fire. ✆ *3 rue du Rey • Map B4 • 02 33 47 70 20 • www.chez.com/campgrav • Closed Nov–Mar • €*

Norman holiday cottage

Price Categories

For a standard, double room per night (with breakfast if included), taxes and extra charges.

€ under €60
€€ €60–€100
€€€ €100–€150
€€€€ €150–€250
€€€€€ over €250

Self-catering Holidays

1 Gîtes de France
The Fédération Nationale des Gîtes de France has more than 2,000 classified properties in Normandy, mostly rural cottages, and should be the first stop for anyone planning a self-catering holiday. ☏ 02 32 62 00 80 • www.gites-de-france-normandie.com

2 French Country Cottages
The UK-based French Country Cottages offers accommodation ranging from small stone cottages to half-timbered houses, or modernized apartments with swimming pools. ☏ 01452 716 830 (UK) • www.french-country-cottages.co.uk

3 Normandie Vacances
The first UK specialist tour operator for the region has been in business for more than 20 years. Their brochure features 120 or so self-catering country houses and cottages, many near the sea and many half-timbered in typical rustic Norman style. ☏ 0845 230 5130 (UK) • www.normandy-holidays.co.uk

4 Allez France
The properties offered by this long-established UK company range from modern apartments to stone or timbered cottages, mostly French-owned. ☏ www.allezfrance.com

5 Pour les Vacances
This French website, where private owners advertise their homes for holiday rental, can be accessed in English. The emphasis is on quality, not quantity. The majority of the properties are handsome, half-timbered Norman cottages or farmhouses. ☏ www.pour-les-vacances.com

6 Welcome Cottages
Based in Lancashire in the UK, Easy Cottages is a branch of Welcome Holidays Ltd. It offers a selection of properties, from modern bungalows to conversions of interesting old buildings. The user-friendly website features exterior and interior shots of each property, as well as detailed descriptions and location maps. ☏ 08452 688 727 (UK) • www.welcomecottages.com

7 French Connections
French Connections arranges special-interest holidays in France, such as painting, walking, climbing, horse riding and language tuition. The majority of their houses in Normandy are owned by private individuals. The website carries full descriptions and photographs of each property and, where possible, provides links with the owner's own website. ☏ www.french connections.co.uk

8 cottages4you
An offshoot of the Holiday Cottages Group, cottages4you has an impressive selection throughout Normandy, details of which appear on its helpful website. With each cottage is a list of all its amenities, as well as a full description of the house and its environs. ☏ 08452 680 760 (UK) • www.cottages 4you.co.uk

9 Discover Normandy
This company lists cottages – more than 120 of them – near a variety of attractions: among others, the D-Day landing sites, golf courses, Mont-St-Michel and beaches. The website includes previous visitors' comments. They will also make your travel arrangements, whether you're going by ferry, train or plane, or want to hire a car. ☏ www.discover-normandy.info

10 Brittany Ferries
As a sideline to their main business, Brittany Ferries arranges self-catering accommodation in a selection of *gîtes*. Although they can't match the choice offered by some of the specialist companies, deals combining ferry travel and accommodation are certainly worth investigating. ☏ 08712 440 439 or 08712 440 744 (UK) • www.brittany-ferries.com

General Index

Acknowledgements

The Authors

Fiona Duncan and Leonie Glass are a British travel-writing team of 15 years standing. They are co-authors of *Top 10 Amsterdam* in the *Eyewitness Top 10 Travel Guides* series, as well as numerous guides for Duncan Petersen, including *Paris Walks* in the *On Foot City Guides* series, and several of the *Charming Small Hotel Guides*. Fiona Duncan is a frequent contributor to the *Daily Telegraph*'s Travel pages.

Produced by DP Services, a division of DUNCAN PETERSEN PUBLISHING LTD, 31 Ceylon Road, London W14 0PY

Project Editor Chris Barstow
Designer Ian Midson
Picture Researcher Lily Sellar
Listings Researcher Dora Whitaker
Indexer Hilary Bird
Proofreader Yoko Kawaguchi

Main Photographer Anthony Souter
Additional Photography Max Alexander, Mike Dunning, Alex Havret
Illustrator chrisorr.com
Maps Dominic Beddow, Simonetta Giori (Draughtsman Ltd)

FOR DORLING KINDERSLEY
Publishing Manager Kate Poole
Managing Editor Fay Franklin
Senior Cartographic Editor Casper Morris
DTP Jason Little
Production Bethan Blase, Melanie Dowland
Design and Editorial Assistance Jane Edmonds, Emer FitzGerald, Anna Freiberger, Christine Heilman, Victoria Heyworth-Dunne, Paul Hines, Laura Jones, Priya Kukadia, Delphine Lawrance, Alison McGill, Alice Reese, Marisa Renzullo, Sands Publishing Solutions, Rachel Symons, Karen Villabona, Dora Whitaker, Lesley Williamson

Picture Credits

Placement Key: a - above; b - below/bottom; c - centre; f - far; l - left; r - right; t - top.

Works of art have been reproduced with the permission of the following copyright holders:

©ADAGP, Paris and DACS, London 2007, *Le Quinze Aôut* (1931) by Raoul Dufy (detail) 48t. ©ADAGP, Paris and DACS, London 2007, *The House* (1907–8) by Georges Braque 49bl.

The publishers would like to thank the following individuals, companies and picture libraries for permission to reproduce their photographs:

AKG-IMAGES: 23c; 40bl; 41br; 50 tl, tr, bl; 51cl, tr; British Library 41tl; Erich Lessing 23b; Gilles Mermet 41tr; ARMADA, ROUEN 2003: 72tl; ASSOCIATION DE TOURISTIQUE L'ABBAYE ROMANE: Pascal Ouine 47bl; 79tr; 80tr; AU SOUPER FIN: 83tl.

BRIDGEMAN ART LIBRARY: The Barnes Foundation, Merion, Pennsylvania, USA, *Le Quinze Aôut* (1931) by Raoul Dufy (detail) 48t ©ADAGP, Paris and DACS, London 2007; Giraudon/Musée Condé, Chantilly, France 11bl; Galerie Daniel Malingue, Paris, France, *The House* (1907–8) by Georges Braque 49bl ©ADAGP, Paris and DACS, London 2007; Giraudon/Bibliotheque Nationale, Paris, France 40tr; Giraudon/ Musee d'Orsay, Paris, France, *The Gleaners* (1857) by Jean-Francois Millet 49br; Giraudon/Musee Marmottan, Paris, France, *Impression: Sunrise, Le Havre* (1872) by Claude Monet 37b; Giraudon/ Priory Church of Brou, Bourge-en-Bresse, France 47cr; Lauros/Giraudon/Musee d'Orsay, Paris, France, *Cathedral in Full Sunlight: Harmony in Blue and Gold* (1894) by Claude Monet 49tr; Musée Crozatier, le Puy-en-Velay, France 40tl; Private Collection/ Peter Willi, *Chemin de la Cavée, Pourville* (1882) by Claude Monet 48cl; Roger-Viollet, Paris 37cr.

C.D.T. MANCHE: 101tr, 102tr; A. Kabacsi 96tl; 100tr; 101tl; P. Lelievre 100tl; CITÉ DE LA MER, CHERBOURG: 52bl; COMITÉ RÉGIONAL DE TOURISME DE NORMANDIE: 56tl, tr cl; H. Guermonprez 62cla; J.F. Lefevre 93tr; COMMISSION POLE TOURISTIQUE DE BESSIN: 29cr; CORBIS: Bernard Annebicque 11br; Bettman 41bl.

DEAUVILLE OFFICE DE TOURISME: 60tr; 70tl.

GÎTES DE FRANCE: 125tl.

FESTIVAL DU CINEMA AMÉRICAIN, DEAUVILLE: 72tr; FONDATION FURSTENBERG-BEAUMESNIL: 91tl.

HULTON ARCHIVE: 31cl.

JARDINS D'ARGENCES: 44cla; JARDINS DE BELLEVUE: 45cr; JARDINS DES PLANTES, ROUEN: 44br; JAZZ SOUS LES POMMIERS, COUTANCES: 72cr.

LA FERME DU CHEVAL DE TRAIT: 111tr; LA TAPISSERIE BAYEUX: By Special Permission of the City of Bayeux 6cl; 12bl; 12-13c; 13t, cb, bl, cr, cbl; 52t; 87c; LES EDITIONS ART LYS: 7br; 34crb; 35tl, cr, clb; LES MUSICALES DE MORTAGNE: 112tr; LES MUSILUMIÈRES DE SÉES: 112tl; LISIEUX OFFICE DE TOURISME: 32cb.

MARY EVANS PICTURE LIBRARY: 15c; 31b; MUSÉE DE LA CÉRAMIQUE, ROUEN: Catherine Lancien, *Buste Apollon* by Nicolas Fouquay 64c; © all rights reserved MUSÉE DES IMPRESSIONNISMES GIVERNY: 36tl; J. Faujour 36tr; MUSÉE DE NORMANDIE, VILLE DE CAEN: 25tl;

MUSÉE ET JARDINS DU CHTEAU DE VENDEUVRE: Musée du Mobilier Miniature 53cl; MUSÉE MALRAUX, LE HAVRE: 53tr.

O.T.I. BAYEUX: 14tr; 55tr; 57tr; OFFICE DE TOURISME OUISTREHAM – RIVA-BELLA: 60bl; ORNE OFFICE DE TOURISME: 106tl.

RESTAURANT GILL: 57bl; ROBERT HARDING PICTURE LIBRARY: 28c; 86cr; Jennifer Fry 8tr; Adam Woolfitt 58br.

SCOPE: Jacques Guillard 67tr; 17cbl; 28crb; 29b; 33cbl; 69tr, br; 71br; 72bl; Noel Hautemanière 33tl, 71cl, 73cr; Francis Jalain 64tr; Franck Lechenet 8cla; SEVEN STORIES PRESS: *A Woman's Story* by Annie Ernaux 51br.

THE NATIONAL ARCHIVES: 15bl.

WELCOME COTTAGES: 133tl; WORLD PICTURES: Wojtek Buss 17bc; Nicholas Holt 58tl; Rex Richardson 88br.

All other images ©Dorling Kindersley. See www.DKimages.com for more information.

Special Editions of DK Travel Guides

DK Travel Guides can be purchased in bulk quantities at discounted prices for use in promotions or as premiums. We are also able to offer special editions and personalized jackets, corporate imprints, and excerpts from all of our books, tailored specifically to meet your own needs.

To find out more, please contact:

(in the United States) **SpecialSales@dk.com**

(in the UK) **travelspecialsales@uk.dk.com**

(in Canada) DK Special Sales at **general@tourmaline.ca**

(in Australia) **business.development @pearson.com.au**

Phrase Book

In Emergency

Help!	**Au secours!**	oh sekoor
Stop!	**Arrêtez!**	aret-ay
Call a	**Appelez un**	apuh-lay uñ
doctor!	**médecin!**	medsañ
Call an	**Appelez une**	apuh-lay oon
ambulance!	**ambulance!**	oñboo-loñs
Call the	**Appelez la**	apuh-lay lah
police!	**police!**	poh-lees
Call the fire	**Appelez les**	apuh-lay leh
brigade!	**pompiers!**	poñ-peeyay

Communication Essentials

Yes/No	**Oui/Non**	wee/noñ
Please	**S'il vous plaît**	seel voo play
Thank you	**Merci**	mer-see
Excuse me	**Excusez-moi**	exkoo-zay mwah
Hello	**Bonjour**	boñzhoor
Goodbye	**Au revoir**	oh ruh-vwar
Good night	**Bonsoir**	boñ-swar
What?	**Quel, quelle?**	kel, kel
When?	**Quand?**	koñ
Why?	**Pourquoi?**	poor-kwah
Where?	**Où?**	oo

Useful Phrases

How are you?	**Comment allez-vous?**	kom-moñ talay voo
Very well,	**Très bien,**	treh byañ
Pleased to meet you.	**Enchanté de faire votre connaissance.**	oñshoñ-tay duh fehr votr kon-ay-sans
Where is/are...?	**Où est/sont...?**	oo ay/soñ
Which way to...?	**Quelle est la direction pour...?**	kel ay lah deer-ek-syoñ poor
Do you speak English?	**Parlez-vous anglais?**	par-lay voo oñg-lay
I don't understand.	**Je ne comprends pas.**	zhuh nuh kom-proñ pah
I'm sorry.	**Excusez-moi.**	exkoo-zay mwah

Useful Words

big	**grand**	groñ
small	**petit**	puh-tee
hot	**chaud**	show
cold	**froid**	frwah
good	**bon**	boñ
bad	**mauvais**	moh-veh
open	**ouvert**	oo-ver
closed	**fermé**	fer-meh
left	**gauche**	gohsh
right	**droit**	drwah
entrance	**l'entrée**	l'on-tray
exit	**la sortie**	sor-tee
toilet	**les toilettes**	twah-let

Shopping

How much does this cost?	**C'est combien s'il vous plaît?**	say kom-byañ seel voo play
I would like ...	**je voudrais...**	zhuh voo-dray
Do you have?	**Est-ce que vous avez?**	es-kuh voo zavay
Do you take credit cards?	**Est-ce que vous acceptez les cartes de crédit?**	es-kuh voo zaksept-ay leh kart duh kreh-dee
What time do you open?	**A quelle heure êtes-vous ouvert?**	ah kel urr voo zet oo-ver
What time do you close?	**A quelle heure êtes-vous fermé?**	ah kel urr voo zet fer-may
This one.	**Celui-ci.**	suhl-wee-see
That one.	**Celui-là.**	suhl-wee-lah
expensive	**cher**	shehr
cheap	**pas cher, bon marché**	pah shehr, boñ mar-shay
size, clothes	**la taille**	tye
size, shoes	**la pointure**	pwañ-tur
white	**blanc**	bloñ
black	**noir**	nwahr
red	**rouge**	roozh
yellow	**jaune**	zhohwn
green	**vert**	vehr
blue	**bleu**	bluh

Types of Shop

antique shop	**le magasin d'antiquités**	maga-zañ d'oñteekee-tay
bakery	**la boulangerie**	booloñ-zhuree
bank	**la banque**	boñk
bookshop	**la librairie**	lee-brehree
cake shop	**la pâtisserie**	patee-sree
cheese shop	**la fromagerie**	fromazh-ree
chemist	**la pharmacie**	farmah-see
department store	**le grand magasin**	groñ maga-zañ
delicatessen	**la charcuterie**	sharkoot-ree
gift shop	**le magasin de cadeaux**	maga-zañ duh kadoh
greengrocer	**le marchand de légumes**	mar-shoñ duh lay-goom
grocery	**l'alimentation**	alee-moñta-syoñ
market	**le marché**	marsh-ay
newsagent	**le magasin de journaux**	maga-zañ duh zhoor-no
post office	**la poste, le bureau de poste, le PTT**	pohst, booroh duh pohst, peh-teh-teh
supermarket	**le supermarché**	soo pehr-marshay
tobacconist	**le tabac**	tabah
travel agent	**l'agence de voyages**	l'azhoñs duh vwayazh

Sightseeing

abbey	**l'abbaye**	l'abay-ee
art gallery	**la galerie d'art**	galer-ree dart
bus station	**la gare routière**	gahr roo-tee-yehr
cathedral	**la cathédrale**	katay-dral
church	**l'église**	l'aygleez
garden	**le jardin**	zhar-dañ
library	**la bibliothèque**	beebleeo-tek
museum	**le musée**	moo-zay
railway station	**la gare (SNCF)**	gahr (es-en-say-ef)
tourist information office	**renseignements touristiques, le syndicat d'initiative**	roñsayn-moñ toorees-teek, sandee-ka d'eenee-syateev
town hall	**l'hôtel de ville**	l'ohtel duh veel

Staying in a Hotel

Do you have vacant room?	**Est-ce que vous avez une chambre?**	es-kuh voo zavay oon shambr
double room,	**la chambre à deux**	shambr ah duh

with double bed	**personnes, avec**	*pehr-son avek*
	un grand lit	*un gronñ lee*
twin room	**la chambre à**	*shambr ah*
	deux lits	*duh lee*
single room	**la chambre à**	*shambr ah*
	une personne	*oon pehr-son*
room with a	**la chambre avec**	*shambr avek*
bath, shower	**salle de bains,**	*sal duh bañ,*
	une douche	*oon doosh*
I have a	**J'ai fait une**	*zhay fay oon*
reservation.	**réservation.**	*rayzehrva-syoñ*

Eating Out

Have you	**Avez-vous une**	*avay-voo oon*
got a table?	**table libre?**	*tabl duh leebr*
I want to	**Je voudrais**	*zhuh voo-dray*
reserve	**réserver**	*rayzehr-vay*
a table.	**une table.**	*oon tabl*
The bill	**L'addition s'il**	*l'adee-syoñ seel*
please.	**vous plaît.**	*voo play*
Waitress/	**Madame,**	*mah-dam,*
waiter	**Mademoiselle/**	*mah-*
		demwahzel/
	Monsieur	*muh-syuh*
menu	**le menu, la carte**	*men-oo, kart*
fixed-price	**le menu à**	*men-oo ah*
menu	**prix fixe**	*pree feeks*
cover charge	**le couvert**	*koo-vehr*
wine list	**la carte des vins**	*kart-deh vañ*
glass	**le verre**	*vehr*
bottle	**la bouteille**	*boo-tay*
knife	**le couteau**	*koo-toh*
fork	**la fourchette**	*for-shet*
spoon	**la cuillère**	*kwee-yehr*
breakfast	**le petit**	*puh-tee*
	déjeuner	*deh-zhuh-nay*
lunch	**le déjeuner**	*deh-zhuh-nay*
dinner	**le dîner**	*dee-nay*
main course	**le plat principal**	*plah prañsee-*
		pal
starter, first	**l'entrée, le hors**	*l'oñ-tray, or-*
course	**d'oeuvre**	*duhvr*
dish of the day	**le plat du jour**	*plah doo zhoor*
wine bar	**le bar à vin**	*bar ah vañ*
café	**le café**	*ka-fay*

Menu Decoder

baked	**cuit au four**	*kweet oh foor*
beef	**le boeuf**	*buhf*
beer	**la bière**	*bee-yehr*
boiled	**bouilli**	*boo-yee*
bread	**le pain**	*pan*
butter	**le beurre**	*burr*
cake	**le gâteau**	*gah-toh*
cheese	**le fromage**	*from-azh*
chicken	**le poulet**	*poo-lay*
chips	**les frites**	*freet*
chocolate	**le chocolat**	*shoko-lah*
coffee	**le café**	*kah-fay*
dessert	**le dessert**	*deh-ser*
duck	**le canard**	*kanar*
egg	**l'oeuf**	*l'uf*
fish	**le poisson**	*pwah-ssoñ*
fresh fruit	**le fruitfrais**	*frwee freh*
garlic	**l'ail**	*l'eye*
grilled	**grillé**	*gree-yay*
ham	**le jambon**	*zhoñ-boñ*
ice, ice cream	**la glace**	*glas*
lamb	**l'agneau**	*l'anyoh*
lemon	**le citron**	*see-troñ*
meat	**la viande**	*vee-yand*
milk	**le lait**	*leh*

mineral water	**l'eau minérale**	*l'oh meeney-ral*
oil	**l'huile**	*l'weel*
onions	**les oignons**	*leh zonyoñ*
fresh orange juice	**l'orange pressée**	*l'oroñzh press-*
		eh
fresh lemon juice	**le citron pressé**	*see-troñ press-*
		eh
pepper	**le poivre**	*pwavr*
pork	**le porc**	*por*
potatoes	**les pommes de**	*pom-duh tehr*
	terre	
rice	**le riz**	*ree*
roast	**rôti**	*row-tee*
salt	**le sel**	*sel*
sausage, fresh	**la saucisse**	*sohsees*
seafood	**les fruits de mer**	*frwee duh mer*
snails	**les escargots**	*leh zes-kar-goh*
soup	**la soupe, le potage**	*soop, poh-tazh*
steak	**le bifteck,**	*beef-tek, stek*
	le steack	
sugar	**le sucre**	*sookr*
tea	**le thé**	*tay*
vegetables	**les légumes**	*lay-goom*
vinegar	**le vinaigre**	*veenaygr*
water	**l'eau**	*l'oh*
red wine	**le vin rouge**	*vañ roozh*
white wine	**le vin blanc**	*vañ bloñ*

Numbers

0	**zéro**	*zeh-roh*
1	**un, une**	*uñ, oon*
2	**deux**	*duh*
3	**trois**	*trwah*
4	**quatre**	*katr*
5	**cinq**	*sañk*
6	**six**	*sees*
7	**sept**	*set*
8	**huit**	*weet*
9	**neuf**	*nerf*
10	**dix**	*dees*
11	**onze**	*oñz*
12	**douze**	*dooz*
13	**treize**	*trehz*
14	**quatorze**	*katorz*
15	**quinze**	*kañz*
16	**seize**	*sehz*
17	**dix-sept**	*dees-set*
18	**dix-huit**	*dees-weet*
19	**dix-neuf**	*dees-nerf*
20	**vingt**	*vañ*
30	**trente**	*tront*
40	**quarante**	*karoñt*
50	**cinquante**	*sañkoñt*
60	**soixante**	*swasoñt*
70	**soixante-dix**	*swasoñt-dees*
80	**quatre-vingts**	*katr-vañ*
90	**quatre-vingt-dix**	*katr-vañ-dees*
100	**cent**	*soñ*
1,000	**mille**	*meel*

Time

one minute	**une minute**	*oon mee-noot*
one hour	**une heure**	*oon urr*
half an hour	**une demi-heure**	*urr duh-me urr*
one day	**un jour**	*urr zhorr*
Monday	**lundi**	*luñ-dee*
Tuesday	**mardi**	*mar-dee*
Wednesday	**mercredi**	*mehrkruh-dee*
Thursday	**jeudi**	*zhuh-dee*
Friday	**vendredi**	*voñdruh-dee*
Saturday	**samedi**	*sam-dee*

Normandy: Selected Town Index